INITIATION RIGHTS

Effective induction practices for new teachers

Peter Earley and Kay Kinder

Published in February 1994
by the National Foundation for Educational Research,
The Mere, Upton Park, Slough, Berkshire SL1 2DQ

© National Foundation for Educational Research

Registered Charity No. 313392

ISBN 0 7005 1357 4

CONTENTS

Acknowledgements		i
Chapter 1	Induction in the 1990s	1
Chapter 2	Effective Induction Practices and Models of Support for NQTs	10
Chapter 3	Early Days (and Late Nights!)	19
Chapter 4	School Induction Programmes and their Managers	28
Chapter 5	School Induction: Assessment and Entitlements	42
Chapter 6	Mentoring: Being All Things to All People?	58
Chapter 7	Mentors in Action	70
Chapter 8	Support from LEAs: Induction Programmes	84
Chapter 9	Support from LEAs: Assessment, Monitoring and Profiling	101
Chapter 10	Managing Induction in Schools	121
Chapter 11	Summary and Concluding Comments	129
References		144
Appendices		146

ACKNOWLEDGEMENTS

The authors would like to thank the teachers and staff of the 30 case study schools and six LEAs who were kind enough to assist in the research project by giving their valuable time to be interviewed on several occasions during the course of the academic year. We hope they think the time was well spent and that the report does justice to both the range of their responses and the insights offered.

Within the NFER, thanks are due to Dr Judy Bradley and Dr Ray Sumner for their helpful comments on an earlier draft of the report, to Pauline Pearce and Alison Bannerman of the Department of Professional Studies and Joan Campbell and Sue Medd of the NFER's Northern Office for their help in the production of this report. We also wish to thank Mary Hargreaves for preparing the manuscript for printing, Tim Wright for the cover design and Enver Carim for overseeing publication of the report.

CHAPTER 1
INDUCTION IN THE 1990s

Introduction

The first 12 months of teaching is generally considered to be not only very demanding but also of considerable significance to the professional development of the new teacher. The experience of the first year is most formative and there is therefore a need to set high expectations and standards when there is greatest receptiveness and willingness to learn and develop. *Induction* – the process which acts as a bridge between training and employment and enables newcomers in any organisation to become effective – can be seen as the first stage in a comprehensive programme of professional support and development available throughout a teacher's career. It is usually defined as the period commencing when an application for a first teaching appointment is successful and concluding, usually after one year, when the newly-trained teacher is considered to have completed a 'probationary' period by demonstrating the necessary expertise to continue in the profession. The induction process should ensure that appropriate guidance, support and training is made available to secure a proper foundation upon which a successful teaching career can be built. It is during the induction period, therefore, that the support of others is crucial if newly-qualified teachers (NQTs) are to develop the competences and confidence that will serve as the base for continuing professional development.

The early 1990s saw a number of significant developments in the induction and support of newly-qualified teachers. In March 1992, Her Majesty's Inspectors published a report which was highly critical of the arrangements found in many schools and local education authorities (LEAs) for the induction and probation of new teachers (GB. DES, HMI, 1992). At the same time, the Secretary of State for Education announced that the statutory one year probationary period for new teachers would be abolished from September, 1992. Previously it had been decided that the main funding mechanism supporting NQTs would be through the Grants for Education and Training (GEST) scheme and LEAs were invited to bid for the category 'the induction of newly-qualified teachers' (GEST Activity 27). In the first year of the scheme (1992-93) 43 LEAs were awarded training grants, whereas in the second and subsequent years all those LEAs who submitted bids were successful. Submissions were invited from LEAs which had to meet certain criteria - criteria which the DFE regarded as leading to more effective practice (see GB. DES, 1992 and Appendix 3).

Probation had not, however, been abolished in Scotland. In fact, December 1991 saw the publication of the findings of a major research study, funded by the Scottish Office Education Department, which documented, *inter alia* the role of the *General Teaching Council (Scotland)* in regulating and overseeing the two-year probationary period (Draper, *et al*, 1991). In the following year the *General Teaching Council for England and Wales* published a document which provided a research perspective on the professional growth of new teachers, along with advice and guidance on the induction of newly-trained and appointed teachers. The GTC also offered a code of practice and some guidelines, which, it was suggested, central government, LEAs and schools should attempt to follow (Calderhead and Lambert, 1992). Finally, in the summer of 1992, HMI as part of their new teacher in school series, undertook a survey of 300 primary and secondary NQTs which investigated the quality of the performance of new teachers, their initial training experiences, and how well they were supported by induction in their first year of teaching (GB. OFSTED, 1993). This survey provided HMI with the opportunity to compare the quality of new teachers' performance in 1992 with that of the previous surveys of 1981 and 1987.

The NFER project

It was against this backcloth of major developments, exhortation and research that the NFER project - *The role of the LEA in the professional development of new teachers* - was undertaken. The project, which lasted 18 months, was funded through the NFER's Membership Programme [1] and commenced in April 1992. In the autumn of that year an interim report entitled *'Beyond Initial Teacher Training: Induction and the Role of the LEA'* documented the results of the first phase of the project (Earley, 1992). This report was based on a questionnaire survey of all LEA personnel with responsibility for induction, seeking information on the organisation of induction, induction programmes, probation and assessment, links with higher education institutions (HEIs), professional development, conditions of service and other matters pertaining to new teachers. Seventy two LEAs completed the questionnaire – a response rate of nearly two-thirds – with most supplying additional relevant documentation, such as the LEA's submission (successful or not) for GEST Activity 27, funding, guidance and handbooks for schools and governors and evaluation reports. (The Executive Summary of the interim report has been included as Appendix 1.)

The interim report of the project was able to provide some important insights into how LEAs were operating in a situation where there were so

---

[1] NFER's members include all the local education authorities, the main teacher associations, some institutes of higher education and various other educational bodies.

many uncertainties surrounding their future role and the function of inspectors and advisers. The ever-changing educational scenario in general, and the abolition of probation and the increased devolution of in-service education and training (INSET) funds to schools in particular, meant that it was becoming increasingly difficult to talk with any degree of precision about the future role of the LEA in relation to the induction and support of new teachers. What was less uncertain, however, was that individual schools – be they LEA – or grant-maintained - would have the *major responsibility* for the induction of teachers new to the profession. In the light of these and other developments, both schools and LEAs are likely to be reconsidering their respective roles in ensuring the smoothest possible transition from initial teacher training through induction to continuing professional development.

The interim report pointed to the variety of ways in which schools and LEAs were working together to support newly-qualified staff. It also recorded a commonly-held concern that the quality of the induction process during the all-important first year of teaching should not be totally dependent upon the school and the degree of importance it attaches to induction. The first phase of the research sought to obtain a national picture of how LEAs, in partnership with schools, were supporting NQTs and the management of school-initiated induction. The interim report, based as it was on a questionnaire survey of advisers and inspectors, could perhaps be perceived as 'a view from the LEA'. In phase two of the research the focus shifted to detailed case studies of *actual* induction practices in schools.

The aim of the second phase of the project was to gather data from school personnel and new teachers on their experiences of the induction process. It was felt that less value would be gained by choosing the case study schools randomly - HMI, for example, had reported that the quality of induction practices was highly variable and less than satisfactory or poor in about one-third of the 42 LEAs and 112 schools they visited between 1988 and 1990 (GB. DES, HMI, 1992) - than by focusing on identified 'good practice'. Further examination of the phase one questionnaire returns and documentation enabled the researchers to draw up a long list of possible LEAs to approach regarding phase two of the research. Further considerations, such as type of LEA, geographical distribution or spread and receipt of GEST funding, resulted in a shortlist being compiled. The relevant LEA personnel were contacted and interviews undertaken which described the purposes of the second phase of the project and requested them to give consideration to schools, which in their view, were successfully managing the induction process. As a result, six LEAs were invited to participate in phase two of the research and, after approaching the schools and obtaining their agreement, they were able to provide the researchers with the names of over 30 schools. (Further details of the 30 schools and six LEAs are provided in Table 1.)

Having obtained information from the LEA personnel about the nominated 'good practice' schools (both primary and secondary), the schools were contacted by the researchers to outline what would be involved and to arrange the first site visit. The schools were informed that the project wished to obtain a picture of induction, largely as experienced by new teachers themselves, over the course of the induction year. As such, the researchers wished to visit each school termly during the course of the academic year. Schools which had several NQTs taking up appointment in September (1992) were requested to select one of these new teachers to participate in the research project. The choice of NQT was made by the school and not by the research team. (In two schools, both employing two NQTs, the researchers were asked to involve both teachers in the research.) Brief background details of the NQTs and their posts are given in Table 1.2.

The visit of the researchers to the schools took place towards the end of *each* term. Interviews were conducted with the identified NQTs, headteachers, induction coordinators/professional tutors, mentors and middle managers. The interviews were semi-structured and sought information on school and LEA induction practices, mentoring and the NQT's progress and development. Relevant documentation (e.g. copies of school induction programmes, advice on observation and visits, school induction policies) was also collected. Approximately 280 interviews were undertaken with school personnel, most of which were taped. The vast majority of interviewees spoke to the researchers on each of the termly school visits. It is this documentary and interview data from the 30 nominated case study schools which form the substance of this research report on effective induction practices. It is hoped that the report will be of great value to all those in schools and LEAs who are involved in the induction of new teachers.

The results of the research are presented in the following sequence. The next chapter attempts to summarise the project's findings in relation to effective induction by discussing the various models of induction support that were found in the case study schools and LEAs. The remaining chapters provide further details of the main forms of school and LEA support. Chapter 3 provides information about the period between successfully applying for a post and taking up appointment. As all of the NQTs involved in the research commenced teaching in September the focus of attention is on the summer period and how that period had been utilised. It also describes how NQTs came to terms with the transition from being a student and gives an indication of how much time was being devoted to school during that first term. The next four chapters focus on school-based induction, particularly induction programmes provided for NQTs and the various 'mentoring' arrangements that were found in the 30 research schools. Chapters 8 and 9 concentrate more specifically on the role of the LEA particularly with reference to central induction programmes, school visits and the production of support materials. Consideration is also given to the attempt by some LEAs to develop profiles to be used by new teachers and their mentors. The following chapter examines the key issues and challenges that were raised in relation to the management of induction in schools. The final chapter provides an overview and a summary of the main findings to emerge from the research and offers brief concluding comments regarding effective induction practices in schools and LEAs.

Table 1.1: Phase 2 Schools & LEAs

	School	Type & age range	No. of teaching staff	No. of NQTs	Coordinator(s) of induction	Other
LEA 1 Outer London borough	1	Comprehensive 11-18	70	4	Professional tutor (DH)	Split site
	2	Comprehensive 11-18	90	6	Professional tutor (Senior Teacher)	Grant-maintained
	3	Infants 4-7	8	1	Professional tutor (DH)	
	4	Junior 7-11	10	1	Professional tutor (DH)	
	5	Infants 4-7	14	2	Professional tutor (Allowance B)	
LEA 2 Metropolitan district (NW)	6	Comprehensive 11-16	92	7	Deputy Head	
	7	Comprehensive 11-16	54	1	Deputy Head	
	8	Primary 4-11	10	1	Mentor (Allowance A)	
	9	Primary 3-11	20	1	DH & Mentor (H of Juniors)	
	10	Primary 3-11	8	1	Mentor (DH)	
LEA 3 Shire County (SE)	11	Comprehensive 12-18	43	4	DH (Mentor)	GEST-funds (92-93)
	12	Comprehensive 12-16	40	4	DH (Mentor)	
	13	Infants 5-8	6	1	HT (Mentor)	
	14	Middle 8-12	15	4	DH & Mentor (Allowance B)	
	15	Primary 5-11	8	1	DH (Mentor)	

Table 1.1: (continued)

LEA 4 Metropolitan district (NE)	16	Comprehensive 11-16	91	4	Deputy Head
	17	Comprehensive 11-16	72	7	Deputy Head
	18	Primary 5-11	18	1	Head
	19	Infants 5-7	9	1	Head & Mentor (Allowance A)
	20	Junior 7-11	14	2	Head
LEA 5 Inner London borough	21	Comprehensive 11-18	62	3	Deputy Head — Single Sex
	22	Comprehensive 11-18	74	6	Induction Coordinator (Senior Teacher)
	23	Primary 4-11	22	2	Induction Coordinator (Allowance C) — GEST-funds
	24	Primary 3-11	9	1	Deputy Head — (92-93)
	25	Primary 4-11	15	2	Head & Induction Coordinator (Allowance B)
LEA 6 Shire County (S)	26	Comprehensive 11-16	70	4	Induction Coordinator (Allowance E) — GEST-funds
	27	Comprehensive 11-16	58	1	Deputy Head
	28	Middle 5-12	14	2	Mentor (Allowance B) — (92-93)
	29	Primary 5-11	9	1	Head & Mentor (Allowance B)
	30	Junior 7-11	20	1	Deputy Head (Mentor)

Table 1.2: Background details of NQTs and their posts

School	Route to QTS	Subject/ Specialism	Age (approx)	Gender	Previous experience	Nature of post	Classes/ subjects taught	Other
1	PGCE	Science	45+	M	Naval engineer	Permanent	11-16 plus 'A' level	Tutor group
2	PGCE	Science	45+	M	Industrial chemist	Permanent	11-16 plus 'A' level	No tutor group (but cover)
3	B.Ed	5-8 yrs	21+	F	First job	Permanent	Mixed age class (5-7)	Appointed from LEA pool
4.	B.Ed	7-11 yrs	21+	F	First job	Permanent	Yr 3 class	Appointed from LEA pool
5a	B.Ed	5-7 yrs	21+	F	First job	Permanent	Yr 2 class	Art Coordinator
5b	PGCE	5-7 yrs	21+	M	First job	Permanent	Yr 1 class	PE Coordinator
6	PGCE	Humanities/RE	21+	M	First job	Permanent	11-16	Optional tutor group / No extra release time
7	B.Ed	Design/Technology	21+	M	First job	Temporary (2 yr contract)	Technology and Home Economics	Tutor group
8	B.Ed	5-11 yrs (Art & Design)	21+	F	First job	Permanent	Yr 1 class	Appointed from LEA pool / Art Coordinator (from Term 3)
9	PGCE	5-11 yrs (History)	25+	M	Private sector	Permanent and abroad	Yr 5 class	Appointed from LEA pool
10	PGCE	7-12 yrs	25+	F	Industry	Permanent	Yr 4 - 5 class	Art Coordinator
11	PGCE	Maths	25+	M	Commerce	Permanent	11-16 plus 'A' level	Appointed from LEA pool
12	PGCE	Humanities	21+	F	First job	Permanent	12-16	No tutor group
13	PGCE	5-12 yrs (Science)	21+	F	Commerce (1yr)	Temporary	Yr 3 class	Appointed from LEA pool
14	PGCE	8-12 yrs (Science)	25+	M	Research (PhD)	Permanent	Yr 5 class	Secretary to school working party
15	B.Ed	5-11 yrs (Health & PE)	25+	F	Commerce	Temporary	Yr 5 class	Post = 2 terms only (Maternity leave)

Table 1.2: (continued)

16	PGCE	Modern Languages	21+	F	First job	Permanent	11-16	Teaching practice (TP) done at school. No tutor group or cover
17	B.Ed	Home Economics/ Technology	35+	F	Parenthood	Temporary	Also teaches IT to Yr 7 class	No tutor group or cover (term 1)
18	PGCE	5-11 yrs (History & English)	21+	F	First job	Permanent	Yr 5 class (team teaches)	Appointed from LEA pool
19	PGCE	5-11 yrs	21+	F	First job	Temporary	Yr 1 class	TP in LEA. Pool appointment & (part) Art Coordinator
20	B.Ed	5-11 yrs (Health & PE)	21+	F	First job	Temporary	Yr 3 class	TP at school (with Mentor) Appointed from LEA pool
21	PGCE	Science	21+	F	First job	Permanent	11-16 plus 'A' level	Tutor group
22	PGCE	Science	35+	M	Commerce & industry	Permanent	11-16 (chose not to teach 'A' level)	Tutor group
23a	B.Ed	4-7 yrs (Maths)	21+	F	First job	Permanent	Reception class	Appointed from LEA pool
23b	PGCE	7-11 yrs	21+	F	First job	Permanent	Yr 1 class	TP at school. Pool appointment
24	PGCE	3-8 yrs	21+	F	First job	Permanent	Yr 6 class	Appointed from LEA pool
25	PGCE	5-11 yrs	25+	F	First job	Temporary	Yr 6 class	Appointed from LEA pool
26	PGCE	Science	21+	M	First job	Permanent	11-16 plus Yr 7 Technology	Tutor group
27	PGCE	Modern Languages	21+	F	First job	Permanent	11-16	No tutor group
28	PGCE	4-8 yrs	21+	F	First job	Permanent	Yr 1 class	Appointed from LEA pool No release
29	B.Ed	8-12 yrs	25+	M	Social work	Permanent	Yr 3-4 class	Appointed from LEA pool No release
30	B.A.	5-11 yrs (Language)	21+	F	First job	Temporary	Yr 6 class	Appointed from LEA pool No release

CHAPTER 2
EFFECTIVE INDUCTION PRACTICES AND MODELS OF SUPPORT FOR NQTs

What is effective induction?

It is often said that the process of induction and any system underpinning it, should ensure that newcomers to a position in an organisation are given the necessary support and guidance to enable them to carry out their duties in an effective manner, whilst also providing a proper base or foundation for their further development. The NFER research was keen to explore participants' views of effective induction and, perhaps unsurprisingly, found a considerable degree of agreement regarding its key features. These usually centred around a number of themes associated with the individual new teacher and/or the organisation or school itself. Induction managers - who were invariably senior staff with a variety of titles (induction coordinator, professional tutor, senior mentor or teacher tutor were the most common) - usually made reference to both schools and NQTs. Effective induction, it was said, would ensure that newly trained teachers or indeed any teacher new to the school felt happy and confident, were team members who saw themselves as part of the school and were willing to contribute to their own development as well as that of the school.

It was not uncommon for respondents to comment on the key features of effective induction by reference to their own experience as probationers - an unhappy experience which several remarked they would not wish on anyone! Individuals spoke of 'being left to sink or swim' and of the potentially damaging effects of such an introduction to the profession. A head of department who was responsible for an NQT in his department remarked:

> *Having worked with unsupportive HoDs I've tried to be supportive, provide materials, advice, 'a shoulder to cry on', and so on. My first school was very large (over 20 in the department). We had a fortnightly meeting but it was insulting and boring. We were thrown in at deep end, the HoD was a time-server! But a HoD doesn't know all the answers and as a new HoD (at this school) I needed support too and we did have some induction as new teachers. In my contacts with the NQT in the department I don't pretend to know all the answers. Sometimes to openly admit that you don't have the answers or you too have problems can be very reassuring to an NQT.* (HoD/Mentor: Secondary.)

Several induction managers and NQTs made reference to the fact that effective induction met the training, development and psychological needs of teachers. Most importantly, it should be seen as something which is **negotiated** between the NQT and the school, rather than being imposed or predetermined. A secondary NQT stressed the **active** role that should be played by the new teacher: *'induction shouldn't be done to you like a ceremony (or initiation rite) you go through, you should be deciding things for yourself?'*

Effective induction was, however, part of a school-wide approach to the support of all staff and would, in general, reflect the culture or ethos found within the school. The quality of relationships amongst staff was crucial and this, to a considerable extent, was a reflection of the culture or ethos the headteacher and other senior managers had been able to create and which permeated the school. Some respondents spoke of the climate of mutual support that had been engendered and how effective induction was part of a broader approach to needs identification which was tailored to the individual teacher:

It has to do with the kind of climate that exists within a school in terms of mutual support amongst the staff. That for me is a very high priority. I think effective induction has to do with the perceived needs of the individual by the individual; I'm not into saying 'I think you should have this or that'. I think that the individual newly qualified teacher needs to be driving force for the kind of induction that takes place within the school and should have the opportunity to be able to say what those needs are and to have those needs listened to. (Headteacher: Primary.)

An NQT in a secondary school similarly, felt that effective induction had to recognise and understand each individual's needs. However:

There has to be recognition that as a newcomer to teaching you might not know what you needs are. So some responsibility must lie with the school and the LEA to predict what those needs could be and then, through individual discussion and negotiation, to decide at what level and how, those needs are to be met. It has to individualised and it has to be an on-going process, not ending after year one. (NQT: Secondary.)

There was a need to create an environment where the new teacher felt comfortable enough to share any problems or strengths and weaknesses they may have had. The key to effective induction was the availability of appropriate support and development systems, which most agreed included such factors as a link to a specific individual (or individuals), a planned programme of classroom observation and feedback, and the opportunity for NQTs to have regular contact with other new teachers, preferably both **within** and **outside** of the host school.

It was most important for the NQT to be able to teach confidently - induction was concerned with providing **personal** support and ensuring that someone was able to identify and deal with any problems or issues at an early stage. Effective induction meant being close and supportive - both in the sense of being trustworthy and in terms of relationships. But more than this it was acknowledged that all teachers needed the opportunity to reflect on their own practice in an honest and meaningful way - induction should therefore lay the foundation for a career based on reflective practice. Although it was acknowledged that NQTs' initial concerns and needs centred heavily around the notion of 'tips for teachers' and survival strategies - and any induction programme should reflect these - this had to be weighed carefully against the school's wider responsibility of preparing someone for a life-long professional career.

There needed to be time created for evaluation and reflection. In the longer term the two had, however, to co-exist for if the NQTs' immediate needs and concerns were not met the chances of continuing professional development, and the critical reflection that underpins such development, were negligible. If induction programmes within schools and LEAs reduced the stress and worry experienced by new teachers then this, in itself, would help them develop professionally much more effectively. Always having someone with whom the NQT could talk in confidence and who was felt to be approachable and supportive was vitally important. The relationship that developed between the NQT and a nominated individual - increasingly referred to as a **mentor** - needed to be one where, as far as possible, NQT's needs and worries were discussed openly and honestly. Effective induction was said to be about making the NQT feel relaxed and comfortable. New teachers should never be made to feel that 'they were on their own' and that support and back up from colleagues was readily available and willingly given.

Effective induction was also about ensuring new teachers saw themselves as active and valued members of staff, able - albeit perhaps to a limited degree - to contribute to the school and its development. A deputy head in a middle school spoke of the need for an NQT to feel they were *'a proper teacher and part of the staff with a role to play'*, whilst a new teacher in another middle-school remarked:

> *It's easy to feel that you are an outsider and it's important that the school asks for your views, especially in relation to important decisions. I have been impressed by the head here because he has felt that our views are important and have affected the decisions made. So it's not only a matter of what the school can do for you but what you can do for the school.*
> (NQT: Middle.)

Respondents remarked that new teachers should be encouraged (like pupils) to realise their potential and be seen as having a valuable contribution to make to the school, the department or year group.

Others spoke of the need to ensure that factors outside of school which may impinge upon a teacher's performance were also considered in any effective induction programme. For example, had the NQTs, been able to find affordable accommodation, transport to school and did they have a social life or a life that went beyond school? Without wishing to pry into the new teachers' personal affairs there was a concern *'about the social side of things'*. Retention too was another hallmark of effective induction and senior managers remarked how, largely as a result of the fact that the school *'looked after their probationers'*, staff had wanted to remain at the school. *'In the past we've not lost people, other than for promotion'*. Secondary headteachers made reference to individual NQTs who had left schools because of the lack of support they had received from middle managers. For one deputy head effective induction was simple: *'did the teacher want to carry on teaching?'* However, this induction manager deliberately made reference to **teaching** rather than *'teaching in this school'* as he perceived a need for the first year to be sufficiently motivating and providing a preparation for the profession as a whole.

In summary, effective induction consisted of a planned but flexible programme of support that encompassed the development of skills, knowledge and expectations - teachers had to have a clear idea of what was expected of them - and observation, both of a by new teachers themselves. New teachers should also be given the time and opportunity to meet with other NQTs. As such, induction of NQTs was not a 'cheap option'; they had to be allocated time and resources. For one NQT involved in the research the question of what constituted effective induction was a simple one: *'it's what we've had so far from the school and the LEA!'*

Although, as this section has demonstrated, there was more or less universal agreement regarding the key features of effective induction, the way in which this expressed itself (in both schools and LEAs) took a variety of forms. The next section explores this in further detail by outlining several models of induction support. The models provide a conceptual framework for a brief discussion of the project's main findings which are explored further in later chapters. However, they should not be seen simply in terms of differing levels or degrees of **effectiveness** - there is no guarantee that the more sophisticated or complex model of induction support is more effective than the simple or basic model. Nevertheless, it is not unreasonable to assume that the former has a greater chance of achieving effectiveness than the latter: as will be shown, the various types and levels of support an NQT benefits from were only rarely achieved by a single individual.

Models of induction support

An attempt to identify models of induction training and support was made in the late 1970s by the Teacher Induction Pilot Schemes (TIPS) project evaluation team (Bolam, *et al*, 1979). On the basis of the data gathered the evaluators described five models of induction training. The fifth - the most complex - was called the White Paper Model and drew heavily on the James' Report (1972) notion of the professional tutor, with a coordinated programme of internal and external support facilitated by the guaranteed release of new teachers (probationers). The NFER research schools and LEAs could only in part have been analysed using the TIPS categories, so it was felt there was a need to provide a framework which could accommodate the full range and complexity of the various structural arrangements and interpersonal processes found in the case study schools and LEAs.

New teachers potentially have a wide range of support, training and development contacts. First, the LEA may provide a central programme of induction - though the amount and timing of this was found to vary considerably. In some LEAs, NQTs received induction sessions for two terms, in others a systematic and regular programme ran throughout the year. Some met once per term, others considerably more frequently. Induction could be subject specific or deal mainly with general issues. The former tended to be ranked highly with secondary NQTs although some saw the value of general sessions. In primary induction programmes age-specific or subject-focused options within an LEA programme were particularly appreciated but again NQTs saw the advantages of general sessions. This arena for interaction with other NQTs was seen as a crucial part of the induction year by virtually all respondents. It was an opportunity for peer support in working through issues, needs and concerns pertaining to the first year of teaching. Above all, LEA induction programmes were highly valued for the practical ideas and suggestions they offered which were seen by NQTs as being capable of immediate implementation.

A second major LEA contribution to induction for the NQT was the advisers' or inspectors' classroom visit. A corollary of the demise of the role of the LEA generally, this input was not a feature in all LEAs. The visit may be from a school/patch inspector or subject adviser (or advisory teacher), and was usually, but not always, connected to a quality assurance function related either to the monitoring of school induction practices or to the assessment of the NQT. In some cases, it related to schools' serious concerns about their NQT's teaching performance. These visits were often valued by NQTs for the 'neutral outsider' role, as well as for insights into teaching performance and foci for development. Senior managers in schools also rated highly the fall-back position which an LEA adviser's observation offered them in the case of 'problem' NQTs. (The LEA's role in providing support and training for NQTs is detailed in Chapters 8 & 9.)

Within schools, NQTs may also experience a central induction programme - meetings held with (or arranged by) senior staff covering a range of issues from the macro-level of school contextualisation to the micro-level of pupil-teacher interaction. Headteachers (in primary), deputy heads or senior teachers usually took responsibility for this aspect of induction support.

The amount and frequency of the school central induction programme meetings again varied: weekly, fortnightly, monthly; in or out of school time (e.g. lunchtime or after school); throughout the year, or first and second terms only. Such formalised meetings were not generally a feature of primary school induction programmes, except in one or two of the larger schools (with more than one NQT). However, meetings organised with subject coordinators did figure in some smaller primary schools.

Opportunities for observation of practice by the NQT - within and outside schools - could also be included in the school's induction programmes at both primary and secondary level. In many instances (though notably less frequently in primary), school induction programmes also included procedures for easing the workload of NQTs. Extra non-contact time, guaranteed no cover arrangements and no- or co-form tutoring (in secondary) were all deliberate management strategies (though cover and form tutoring may be instituted later in the year). New teachers in primary schools were not usually expected to take on a curriculum or subject coordinator responsibility in their first year, although both school induction managers and NQTs themselves expected such responsibilities in their second or subsequent years. However, a small number did take responsibility for the coordination of foundation subject (PE and art). Staff responsible for induction often had an assessment function. (School induction programmes and the various ways in which support is provided by schools is discussed in Chapter 4 and 5.)

School induction programmes may also begin in the summer term prior to the NQT taking up their teaching post - with considerable variation in the amount of structured support offered to the NQT at that time, the kinds of information relayed and how much time the NQT spent in school. Payment to the NQT for summer induction was sometimes a feature. (Chapter 3 provides examples of how the summer period can usefully be used.)

A further dimension to the support systems for NQTs was invariably that of the 'mentor'; someone within the school offering one-to-one support relating to classroom practice, curriculum planning and/or administration. Mentors could be of varying status, usually middle management, though heads, deputies and ex-probationers might also carry the nomenclature. Mentor involvement with NQT assessment was another variable. In some cases, a second 'mentor' was instituted, often of lower status who operated in non-judgmental mode. The relationship might be formalised by regular and timetabled tutorials, or mentors might operate in responsive mode. It may follow the procedure and agenda of LEA profiles (usually competence-based) and developed, using GEST funds, in conjunction with institutes of higher education (HEIs). (See Chapters 6, 7 and 9 for further details of mentoring arrangements and NQT profiles.)

Put together, the NQT's arenas of support are shown in Figure 2.1.

Figure 2.1: Arenas of support for NQTs

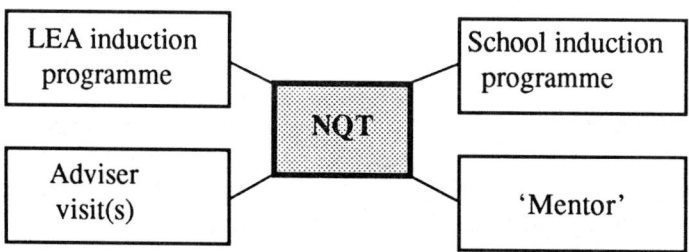

However, two further networks were possible. Education authorities could offer mentor training and/or support groups, most often to those with responsibility for induction, though sometimes to middle managers with mentoring responsibilities. Alternatively, or as well, written guidance in the form of handbooks, and/or guidelines to the profile were made available. Equally (though this was rare), school induction coordinators could offer training/support to their own staff in cases where a number of mentors were operating in the school.

Four main models of induction support emerged within the case study schools:

- *Mono-support systems*

In this system, responsibility for an NQT's induction was officially undertaken by a single person, usually in a senior management role. No other person from within school had a formal or official input into induction. However, informal support might be offered or sought from other personnel (e.g. headteachers, year colleagues) and official assessment functions undertaken by the headteacher or another senior staff member. This system more usually operated where a single NQT was appointed and was more common in primary than secondary schools.

- *Bi-support systems*

In this system, the school offered support from 'a mentor' (usually of middle management status such as a departmental head) in addition to a central induction programme involving the provision of information on school procedures and/or opportunities for discourse on teaching and learning issues. The latter was operated by senior management in the role of coordinator of induction; the central programme may also involve tutorial support.

The pre-eminence of one or other of these two arenas of support was a significant variable. Thus, the mentor relationship might have formal prominence - usually signalled by timetabled meetings and/or the following of profile procedures. Sometimes, the mentor's strong personal commitment to the NQT's development was evident without these formal accoutrements. In some other examples of bi-support systems, the school's central programme emerged as the main source of induction support; with a less defined, committed or consistent role for the mentor. In these cases, the induction manager or coordinator might make a strong pastoral commitment to the NQT. Alternatively, both levels of support might be a particularly strong feature.

- *Tri-support systems*

Tri-support systems usually offered a combination of central meetings and/ or supervision (involving senior staff), middle management mentor support (academic and/or pastoral) and, as well, another official designated personnel of similar or near similar status, such as a 'buddy', a 'critical friend', a second i/c or year leader. This extension to the support system was being formally instituted in more than one school for the following academic year as the overlap of assessment and support functions for official mentors sometimes proved problematic (see Chapter 6 and 7).

- *Multi-support systems*

Multi-support systems referred to those school induction programmes which offered support at a number of levels (either as bi- or tri-support systems), but in addition had evidence of coordination between the levels. Thus, school induction managers running training and information sessions for mentors in their schools would be an example of a multi-support system. An example from the primary school sample was where a headteacher attended the planning meetings of the NQT's year group and the mentor attended the school's central sessions along with the NQT. Again, there was evidence of some schools adapting their induction procedures to a multi-support system, as the need for consistency between mentors emerged. However, there were no examples of mentors contributing to secondary school central programmes. Joint training of mentors/NQTs featured in one LEA but appeared not be adopted in schools, despite several assertions by mentors and NQTs of the value - and logic - of this.

The remainder of this report of the second phase of the NFER project provides further details and gives examples of schools operating within the main models of induction support. A three-dimensional representation of the multi-support system for the induction of NQTs is offered in Figure 2.2.

Figure 2.2. Multi-support system for the induction of NQTs

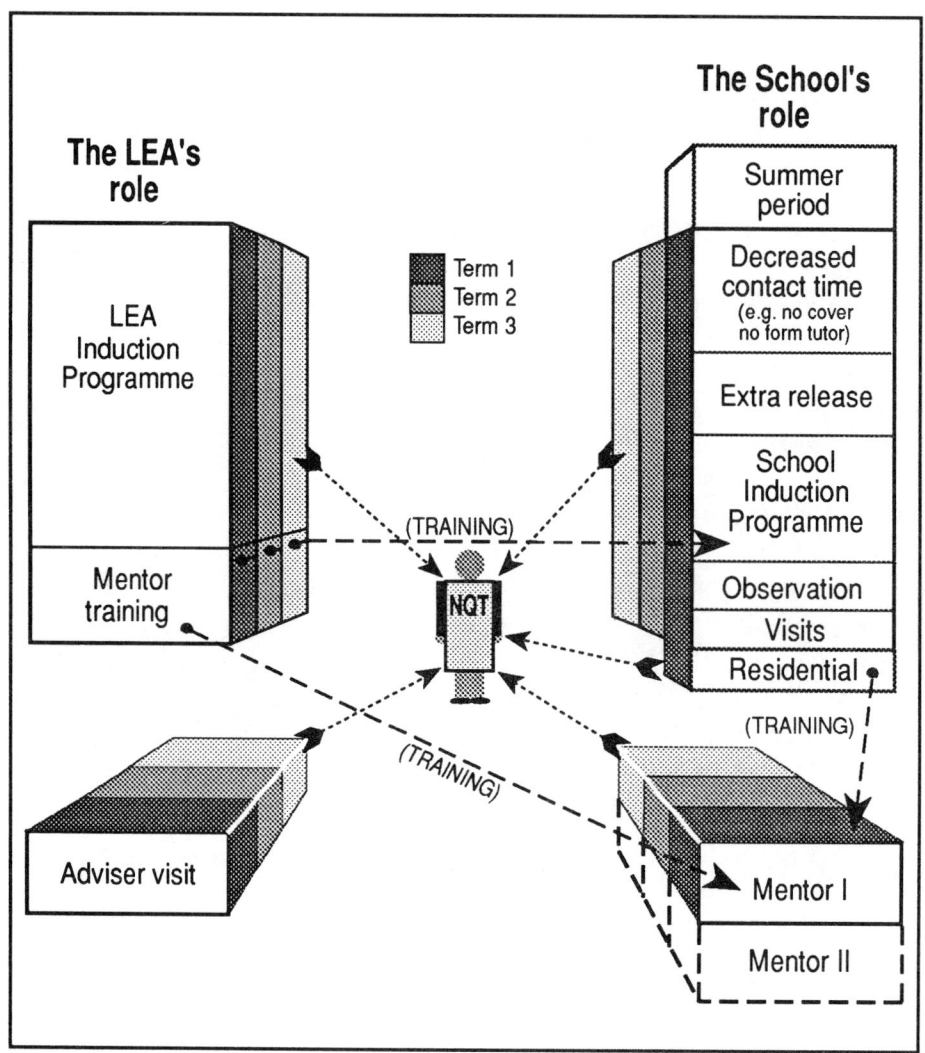

CHAPTER 3
EARLY DAYS (AND LATE NIGHTS!)

In England and Wales the vast majority of new teachers are appointed to take up their first position at the beginning of the academic year (September). The induction process itself, however, is often seen to commence at the time of appointment and to continue throughout the first year of teaching. As part of the NFER project, data were obtained from NQTs and others on the preparations made during the summer before commencing work, although NQTs' experiences of the appointment process itself were not documented.

An important part of the research was to explore with NQTs (both during the initial interviews in term 1 and the final interviews in term 3) their experiences of the summer period and the degree to which they were subject to 'culture' or 'transition shock' during those all-important first few days and weeks. The research also wished to explore the degree to which NQTs perceived induction as important when applying for posts and, once in post, the approximate amount of time they were devoting each week to the school and the new job. This chapter draws upon these data to consider the NQTs' experiences during the summer and in their first term in post.

Information and guidance to schools on what should be made available to NQTs, including opportunities to visit and documentation offered **before** taking up appointment, has recently be issued by the DFE (GB. DES, 1992) and by the *General Teaching Council for England and Wales* (Calderhead and Lambert, 1992). Data from the NFER questionnaire survey showed that the vast majority of LEAs provided some form of written guidelines or handbooks to their schools which usually included a summary of such documents (see Appendix 1). All of the six case study LEAs involved in the second phase of the project provided schools and NQTs with such documentation. During the course of the research, one of the LEAs, with GEST funding, produced an information pack for schools which included a section on establishing a programme of induction and support for the new teacher. Within this section the nature and type of support required was described in five phases. These are outlined in Figure 1 and the first two phases are of particular relevance as they deal with the period between appointment and taking up the post, and those first few weeks when the school is in session. (The induction and support programme over these five phases has, with the permission of the case study LEA, been reproduced in full in Appendix 2.)

Figure 1   The induction sequence

- Phase 1 - commences when the NQT is appointed

- Phase 2 - a period of adjustment for NQTs as they join the staff of the school

- Phase 3 - a period of developing relationships - throughout the first half term - as NQTs settle into school routines

- Phase 4 - a period of consolidation, lasting as it does up to the beginning of the final half-term of the induction year

- Phase 5 - at the end of the induction year, it is important that NQTs continue to receive support as required and plans made for continued professional development

Job applications: does induction matter?

At the time when the NQTs involved in the research were applying for teaching posts (Spring 1992) it was announced that the probationary year was to be abolished. Most NQTs remarked that their college and university tutors had made reference to this future development, whilst several tutors had suggested that information on induction be sought at interview, as the amount of support offered would vary considerably both within and between schools and LEAs. Just under one-third of the NQTs involved in the NFER project stated that induction was **not** mentioned at all during the course of their initial teacher training. One respondent had been made aware of induction as the probationers at her teaching practice school were involved in a common induction programme with students, whilst another remarked how an LEA adviser had visited her HE institution to talk to the entire PGCE group about the induction support currently available in the LEA.

The new teachers participating in the NFER research were also asked if induction was important to them when they were applying for teaching posts. The earlier survey of local authority personnel had found that over three-quarters of respondents regarded the availability of an LEA induction programme as an important incentive for NQTs when applying for posts. Indeed, when interviewed at the end of the project, one of the case study LEA induction coordinators remarked that their own enquiries had revealed that about one-half of the NQTs had been attracted to the LEA because of its highly regarded induction programme. Interestingly, about one-half of the NQTs interviewed across the six case study LEAs remarked that induction was **not** an important factor and that other factors, such as geographical location or the school itself, were more significant. For some

– perhaps a growing number in the light of the decreasing employment opportunities for teachers – of most importance was simply to secure an appointment. As one primary NQT remarked: *'the job situation this year has been very tight. Getting a job was of more importance (than induction) and I didn't want to rock the boat.'* Another commented:

> *I didn't think to ask about induction at the interview - your mind is full of what you can offer the school not the other way round - though I realise how important it is, especially when I hear of the non-support some of my fellow NQTs get!* (NQT: Secondary.)

For one of the NQTs, induction was considered extremely important as a result of an assignment he had completed at college, whilst another remarked that although induction was not particularly significant in accepting the post, the fact that a comprehensive programme was mentioned, suggested to him that the school might also be well-organised in other areas. Several NQTs remarked that they were pleased to discover a programme of induction support was to be made available to them as they were very conscious of the need to continue to learn. As one noted: *'simply because you've finished your training doesn't mean that learning stops.'*

Easing the transition

The degree to which new teachers experience a 'transition' or 'culture shock' as they transfer from being students to becoming NQTs will, of course, be affected by a number of factors. The training they have received, their preparations and visits to the new school in the summer, and individual personality factors are perhaps the most obvious. When asked about the transition, just under one-half of the NQTs remarked that a culture shock had been experienced, albeit to varying degrees. For some there was 'a big jump' between what they had learned in college (and on teaching practice) and what was expected of them as 'real' teachers. As one four year trained teacher explained:

> *It was a big shock because I'd never been in a class before from September with a new class and you had to sort out everything. When I was doing my teaching practice there were a lot of things that were done for you, the grouping, the abilities, etc. You never got to see a class at the beginning of the year. This would have been helpful because when you go in you think it's easy but you don't realise how much has gone before to get the children to that stage. The transition shock was real, you don't realise until you actually experience it.* (NQT: Primary.)

A teacher who had benefited from having done her PGCE teaching practice at the case study school spoke similarly of experiencing a culture shock:

> *Yes, everybody does (experience shock), though I was at an advantage with knowing the school. The (nearly) full time-table, doing duty, attending extra pastoral meetings and staff meetings is what causes the culture shock. With TP, you didn't do all those things and you knew it was going to end; it's short-term... the 19 days to go (syndrome).*
>
> (NQT: Secondary.)

In one case, it was difficult to get used to the routine of a timetable after four years as a B.Ed. student, whereas for others the transition was not so great after the 'intensity of the PGCE'. The NQTs who had worked outside of education provided some interesting remarks on how teaching was different from other jobs they had previously held. One commented that teaching was the most difficult job he had ever taken on, whilst another pointed to the degree of responsibility that was given from the outset. In this sense any training received 'can only take you so far'.

The methodological approach adopted in the research did not make it possible to state unequivocally if there was an inverse relationship between the degree of discomfort experienced and the preparations and visits made over the summer. It can be said, however, that most of those NQTs *not* experiencing shock stressed the importance of the summer period and how they had most usefully spent time familiarising themselves with the new school, its procedures, pupils and staff. All the NQTs involved in the research were able to visit their schools during the summer, although the amount of time spent on-site varied considerably, as did the way in which that time was utilised. Benefits gained were also said to vary. However, only a few regarded their summer experiences as unproductive. A one-year trained science teacher who had found the transition from student to teacher to be smooth remarked:

> *In the summer I spent a week in school and I think more could have been made of it. We were put into our department and there wasn't a lot that they could do for us - probably because of lack of time of other teachers. I taught a couple of lessons, but you weren't under any pressure and you didn't pick up a proper feel of the school. It left me slightly bewildered - I didn't understand the timetable, what I would be teaching, etc. I would have liked somebody (e.g. HoD) to have taken us in-hand and said this is what you are teaching, syllabuses, etc., so that for rest of holidays you could have prepared yourself. I didn't know the subject matter or anything at all. I felt 'my gosh in six weeks time I'll be teaching and I've got nothing prepared!'*
>
> (NQT: Secondary.)

A secondary teacher in a different LEA was similarly unimpressed with the three (unpaid) half-day visits he had made to his department. He had not been given his schemes of work (they did not arrive until the day before he was due to start teaching) and would have liked the opportunity to have met his mentor, other heads of department (in his teaching area) and for some time to be spent on school rules. The handbook he had been given was 'too big to absorb'.

The amount of documentation to make available to NQTs was an important consideration for the case study schools. In one school where the NQT was in receipt of 'a hefty handbook' it had formed the topic of the school's central induction programme in the third week of term ('The School Handbook: Your Questions Answered'). Induction managers were conscious of the need to obtain the right balance of information and not to overload the NQT with unnecessary detail. In a few cases a 'Welcome Pack' or an induction manual were offered and in one primary school a handbook with alphabetical listings (e.g. A for Attendance, W for Wet Play) was considered to be most helpful. Building up relationships, reassurance and friendship were of paramount importance and were said to outweigh the need for copious documentation. As one primary head remarked: *'We have given him a minimum amount of documentation and this will increase as and when needed. If he needs to know something then hopefully he will not be afraid to ask.'*

NQTs preferred not to be overwhelmed by documentation; nevertheless they did not like things to be left to chance. In some cases NQTs reported being unsure about certain matters, yet reluctant to ask staff members. In such instances and where possible, it was found useful for the school to provide opportunities during the summer visits for the NQT to be introduced to teachers about to complete the induction (or probation) period. As one new teacher commented:

being introduced to last year's (probationer) was very helpful because she was able to tell me some of the little things that very often other people forget. For example what form to fill in for detention, what the strange symbols on the timetable meant and so on. (NQT: Secondary.)

It was common for NQTs to spend several days in the school during the summer with most schools offering an unstructured and informal programme. The following extract from a headteacher interview illustrate the sorts of activities that occurred:

After the interview, she was invited to school and came in on two or three occasions. We gave her all the available advice - (e.g. Programmes of Study for Maths); and the school policies: the NQT had the opportunity to talk with her class's current teacher; to look at their books - and was told areas of curriculum she'd cover content wise - there was not much they could tell her on the precise needs of the children, level wise and she couldn't take the records because they were being worked on. We tried to make her feel that nothing was a problem - we all have them - if you share it we can help you, if you hide it, we can't. This was a lot more than we'd done the year before, even though it might not be much!

(Headteacher: Primary.)

New teachers were also strongly encouraged to attend school INSET or professional development days which often occurred towards the end of the summer term. There was an expectation on the part of senior staff that NQTs would want to visit the school in the summer but differing views were held on whether payment for such visits should be made.

Most primary NQTs took the opportunity in the summer to familiarise themselves with the class they would be taking in the new academic year. In a few cases NQTs were spending up to three weeks (unpaid) in this familiarisation process. Generally this was seen as time well-spent. However, in one instance a decision was made by the NQT to visit the school but **not** to observe her future class. This person wanted to retain her status as a teacher and felt she would inevitably lose it by having to talk with the children informally, whilst her role was 'still ambiguous'. Another remarked how she would have liked to have taught 'her' children in small groups, for a week, with the existing teacher still in the classroom. It was also felt to be important to have the opportunity to observe different classes and many of the more structured summer induction programmes included elements of this, such as a pupil pursuit.

It is worth noting that several respondents remarked that although opportunities to visit schools were worthwhile, it was often the case that life in schools in the summer was hectic and 'not very typical'. In some schools it was difficult for senior staff to find the time (let alone 'quality time') or the resources for the new teachers. Also several comments were made about the unsuitability of offering supply work to NQTs unless a very light timetable was guaranteed.

Formally structured summer induction programmes were found in only three schools. Brief details of each are given below along with comments from NQTs about their perceived value.

Summer induction programmes: three examples

Example 1: A secondary school

Six NQTs had been appointed to this grant maintained school and were invited to participate in a two-week pre-appointment induction programme. They were paid £250 for one week (in the past probationers were paid for two weeks) and also for the month of August (although this was unlikely to continue 'in the light of market forces'). The programme was sent to the NQTs in advance and each NQT asked to complete a personal profile so the school (and LEA) knew precisely what had been covered during training and could therefore plan a programme accordingly over the induction year. Each NQT received a loose-leaf, colour coded school handbook covering such things as school aims, routines, resources, pastoral structure, exams and finance. For two weeks in July a timetabled programme was organised for the new teachers which was both department-based and school-wide. It included: a school training day, NQT training, reflection time, an activity, exploring the school, a pupil pursuit and work in departments. In addition, one day was spent at the LEA Teachers' Centre where NQTs met up with other new teachers and were given an outline of the induction support and resources that would be made available to them. The professional tutor also had a session in the summer term with those HoDs with NQTs to go over their roles and responsibilities ('All my best laid plans fall down if the HoDs don't do what they're supposed to!')

The NQT interviewed in this school was most appreciative of the support provided by the school and the LEA. He remarked that pay was a bonus ('I'd have come in anyway') and that the two weeks 'were useful if a bit long'. Time was spent in the department 'but people were very busy'. More useful was the time he was able to spend outside the department, especially the observation of teachers not in his subject area which occurred through the pupil pursuit. He remarked: 'I felt quite well prepared and ready to start in September. The programme was very relevant and worthwhile'.

Example 2: A primary school

Two NQTs had been appointed to this inner-city school from the LEA 'pool'. As soon as the NQTs were appointed they were invited to visit the school. The purpose of the first day's visit was really just to say 'hello' and introduce them to the school. The school then followed the LEA's recommendations and suggested they spend a whole week in the summer, being employed on supply rates. They were also given a £500 'golden hello'. The head remarked: 'I think it's well worth finding that money. It's a hangover from the days of recruitment difficulties but I'd still want to do it because it's a statement that the school cares about its NQTs. This money is taken from the school's delegated budget. It's a case of valuing people.'

During the week in the summer, time was spent with each curriculum co-ordinator, going through NC documents, school policies and schemes of work and planning their first half-term project. Resources were shown and NQTs also met their teacher tutor (responsible for induction) who helped them with their first project. By the end of the week the NQTs knew in some detail what they would be teaching in the first half term, so they were able to spend part of the holidays, if they wished, on getting ready. 'It's really important they go in on that first day knowing exactly where they are'. (The school paid for the supply cover during the summer week.) Also, on several occasions, the NQTs planned with their parallel class teacher and there was a tour of the local area. They were made aware of their mentor/buddy who was likely to be their neighbour and would help them get through the routines of the school. They also received a detailed induction handbook (policies, schemes of work, school routines, etc.) The head asked staff if they would act as 'mentors'; ideally the mentor would be the teacher taking the parallel class. 'The NQT should know them quite well because they will have planned their first topic together'. The school was also aware of the NQTs' accommodation needs and tried to help (as did the LEA) as 'this can be a great worry'. The NQT interviewed in this school found the week's programme very valuable. She also came into the school for two days over the summer holidays and felt that she had settled in quite well. As a result of the programme of meetings (with staff and pupils) and visits, along with the documentation received, she felt 'a lot more relaxed' over the holiday. 'Friends of mine who have not had that (week in the summer) have had a much more difficult time settling in. Getting to know the staff makes a big difference'. This NQT also added that it was a bonus to have been paid for the week.

Example 3: A secondary school

Four NQTs had been appointed to this school which had an induction policy stating that **before** appointment NQTs had certain entitlements, such as the opportunity to visit the school, meet colleagues, obtain a timetable and receive appropriate year group, faculty and department information as well as details of the school and LEA's programme of induction support. Interestingly, the pre-appointment induction programme had been revised in the light of the NQTs' and other comments. Next year's ten new teachers (six NQTs and four others) were to be offered a two-day programme which had been organised by the deputy head i/c induction. The deputy stated that the two-day programme was to build them into a team 'so they'll share experiences more readily in the school central induction programme'. They could finalise another visit for further information/timetables etc., but the deputy ensured all information (on procedures, systems, schemes of work, etc) was given out during those two days. The pre-appointment induction period was seen as expressing to the NQTs the support and commitment of the school to **their** induction, but also it was to encourage them to actively seek help/ support where necessary.

The actual programme consisted of:
Day 1: (with deputy) tour of school; introduction to key staff, office and support staff, office procedures explained; reprographics (shown and explained). Staff room for coffee at break. Session, in DH's room explaining: support systems for NQTs, feedback on previous NQT's comments e.g. be pro-active in gaining help. Lunch in pub. Minibus tour for a view of catchment area, visit feeder primary schools, meet some Y6 pupils (ie. future Y7). One hour session with Head of Upper and Lower School on pastoral provision. Documentation on school procedures/ systems given (e.g. if you're late) in a pack the DH had developed.

Day 2: (in their departments) observing, schemes of work given plus lunch with department organised. Met again at end of day with DH to provide future access opportunities (telephone numbers over holidays, how to arrange further visits). Travelling expenses for these two days were paid by the school. Feedback from the NQTs was positive: the new teachers said they felt more part of the school and had already struck up positive relations with each other.

It can only get easier!

Her Majesty's Inspectors in their survey of 300 new teachers in the summer of 1992 asked teachers to estimate the amount of time they spent on their work and found the total working week to be about 50 hours (GB. OFSTED, 1993). The new teachers participating in the NFER research were similarly requested to give an indication of the amount of time each week they were devoting to the school. The responses were remarkably consistent with virtually all stating that they worked an eight or nine hour day with marking, preparation and other tasks undertaken in the evenings and weekends. A 50 hour week was not uncommon with many spending considerably more time, especially at peak times in the term. Obviously events such as forthcoming parent evenings, the completion of pupil records of achievement and reports were important factors, as was whether or not the NQT had a form tutor group or taught a range of different classes and subjects (some of which they might not have been trained for). A mature teacher who taught science remarked:

> *It's not hard intellectually but it's just never-ending: teaching, marking, planning. It's a long (autumn) term and you are always having to set and mark topic tests and do ROAs, etc. You are just getting on top when you're asked to do reports (on pupils you hardly know!) or mark some exams. You suddenly realise there's even more to do. You just get in a position to look ahead when this happens! The screws are turned even more. It's difficult for everyone but particularly for NQTs who don't know enough - we have to look up everything. Yes, I do have a form tutor group. I would have liked not to have one or to have shared one. The split site doesn't really help either.* (NQT: Secondary.)

Several NQTs remarked how they had been advised by their mentors, teacher tutors or induction coordinators to devote less time to the school - to 'switch off', to have 'another life outside of school' or to ensure that at least one day at the weekend was spent 'not doing school-work'. Time spent away from the job was seen as vital to the mental well-being of the new teacher and several remarked how the job was 'on your mind all the time'. Other NQTs commented how their own work-load, although demanding, had been considerably reduced by the amount of joint planning that occurred in their school or department.

Some NQTs had deliberately not volunteered for anything in their first year of teaching and were very conscious of the need 'not to overstretch yourself'. There was a general awareness that teaching was 'not an easy option' but with more experience, greater familiarity and better time management, things could only improve. Nevertheless, at the time of the third research visit, several NQTs were asking serious questions of themselves and their choice of career: they were not sure if they were prepared 'to give up their lives to teaching' as had been necessary in their first year in the profession.

CHAPTER 4
SCHOOL INDUCTION PROGRAMMES AND THEIR MANAGERS

The central focus of the following two chapters is the role that the school plays in the induction process. This chapter commences with an analysis of the managers of induction before giving detailed consideration to the central induction programmes the case study schools provided for their NQTs. Chapter 5 continues to look at school-based practices and gives attention to the observation of NQTs for assessment purposes, school-based mentor training and to the important role induction managers play in administering NQTs' rights and entitlements.

The managers of school induction

This section examines the status and responsibilities of those staff who take on a school-wide coordinating brief with regard to the induction of new teachers. On this aspect of induction there is considerable variation between primary and secondary schools, largely because the former more usually appoint only one (or two) NQTs at any one time, whereas, as the research showed, it was fairly common for the secondary schools to be inducting four or more NQTs in any one year. Formal induction programmes might, quite naturally, figure less prominently when the focus is on only a single individual.

The first issue to explore, however, was who took responsibility for induction in the school, and Tables 4.1 and 4.2 give a breakdown of personnel who, in the course of the project's initial fieldwork visit, were nominated as having the title 'induction coordinator' or, more generally (as was often the case in primary schools), having 'overall charge' of the NQT's induction. For the purposes of this chapter, those carrying formal responsibility are given the title 'induction manager'. The tables distinguish between:

- personnel who have overall induction responsibility (induction manager); and

- those who have a designated official mentoring role as well as this overall induction responsibility (induction manager plus mentor)

Table 4.1 Personnel with induction responsibility: secondary schools

	Induction manager + mentor	Induction manager	Total
Deputy Head	2	7	9
Senior Teacher	0	3	3
Total	2	10	12

Table 4.2: Personnel with induction responsibility: primary schools

	Induction manager + mentor	Induction manager	Total
Deputy Head	1	8	9
Senior Teacher	4	2	6
Allowance 'C'	1	0	1
Allowance 'B'	1	1	2
Total	7	11	18

A first general - and fairly obvious - point from Tables 4.1 and 4.2 is the fact that induction responsibility/coordination remained very much the remit of senior management in both the primary and secondary case study schools. The exceptions were in three primary schools where teachers holding 'B' and 'C' allowance posts (hence middle managers) were nominated as induction coordinators. However, in one case the teacher with the allowance also had an LEA-wide induction support role and therefore demonstrable expertise, if not overt status, to take on induction responsibilities. In another, the teacher with the allowance worked as a year group leader with designated responsibility for five other staff, including the school's two NQTs, in her year - hence a management role of some import was already evident. (This teacher was the only primary middle manager to take on an induction responsibility without an accompanying mentor role: the NQTs were asked to select two other year group members as their 'buddy' mentors once the term had started.) Interestingly, by the end of the school year, in the third primary school with a middle manager as induction coordinator, the headteacher suggested, in future, induction responsibility would be assigned to the deputy head, thus conforming to the general perception that senior staff should oversee induction.

It is also noticeable that, with only one exception, all the primary school sample's deputy heads with any official induction management role were non-class based for at least the initial term of the school year.

In the secondary school sample, deputy heads very frequently took on the role of 'induction coordinator', though in three cases the responsibility was delegated to a senior teacher (typically, they might carry an 'E' allowance and be on a 60 per cent timetable). Two of these senior teachers had direct responsibility for initial teacher training as well as induction. There was only one instance of a secondary middle-manager with a school-wide induction role: one deputy head reported involving a middle management colleague - an ex-head of year - (who was also working in the school's ITT programme) as a support for the NQTs' central induction sessions. This person, designated 'tutor-mentor/pastoral-mentor', was already undertaking mentor training for ITT work, and later in the year was reported as having led some of the central induction sessions and undertaken some observations of the NQTs.

A second point to emerge from Tables 4.1 and 4.2 is the number of induction coordinators who also carried a mentoring brief, this was especially evident in primary schools. Increasingly, a number of these (and one of the secondary deputies with the same designated dual role) doubted their capacity to take on **both** these aspects of induction.

> *It shouldn't be the case that headteachers are mentors as well - heads are heavily involved in managerial issues which take them away from the classroom and school. Overall responsibility might rest with the head, but there are time constraints and a limit to the support they can provide. That [classroom] side of NQT support should be delegated.*
> (Mentor: Primary.)

> *I have delegated induction responsibility to the DH but ... next year, in this school in order to improve practice, we will move the deputy's role of mentor to somebody else. This is because his responsibilities are many and diverse, the demands on him are really too many.*
> (Headteacher: Primary.)

> *The administrative overview of induction should be done at deputy level because getting staff off timetable and making sure NQTs have access to resources needs clout, but the person who should be their mentor in the truest sense is the person to whom they're directly responsible - at department level.* (Mentor/DH: Secondary.)

This issue of appropriate mentor status will be explored in more detail in Chapter 6. However, it would seem that, regardless of the size of the institution, the overall responsibility for induction is almost invariably seen as appropriately associated with the school's most senior staff.

That being the case, it is interesting to tabulate the length of time which this sample of 'induction managers' had actually been undertaking their responsibility in the school. In the initial interview at all 30 case study schools, each nominated person with induction responsibility (whether it be a primary head or a secondary senior teacher) was asked how long they had been carrying out the role. Table 4.3 indicates their responses.

Table 4.3: **Length of time with induction responsibility (in present school)**

	Primary: N=18	Secondary: N=12	Total
Less than one year	1	8	9
1 - 2 yrs	4	2	6
3 - 4 yrs	1	0	1
5 -10 yrs	1	1	2
More than 10 yrs	1	1	2

Thus, more than half of the sample (17 out of 30) had been responsible for induction for only two years or less, and about a quarter (seven out of 30) were in their first year as induction manager. This finding, in a sample of schools selected because they were thought to illustrate good practice, is perhaps surprising. It may suggest that investment in the role itself is a recent component of senior management responsibilities or, even more, features as a fairly recent **construct** within management thinking.

This school is very hierarchical and always had senior management as the supervisor of NQTs. Until my appointment, this person only monitored or administered them, rather than looked after them. I hope I've changed that aspect, brought a human face to the senior role.
(Induction coordinator: Secondary.)

This high number of recent appointments may also suggest a new or renewed formal commitment to induction by the school, as the devolvement of staff development responsibilities to schools generally gathers pace. However, at the same time, without a strong tradition of induction management evident in the sample, it is possible to conclude that the parameters of the role may as yet be fairly undefined. Looking at the types of activity which induction managers in both the primary and secondary school samples undertook, it was evident that there was considerable variation in the way they operated, and the amount of time invested in the role.

Several different modes of activity were evident across the sample of schools, with many of the induction managers operating in more than one mode:

- organising and/or convening a central programme of induction
- undertaking individual interviews/tutorials with their NQT(s)
- undertaking the observation and assessment of the NQT
- coordinating the activity of the teaching staff designated as mentors

Another, essentially administrative, aspect of the role was also mentioned by a number of induction managers. This did not necessarily involve interaction with the personnel directly supporting or receiving induction but can be included in modes of responsibility:

- overseeing/ensuring the NQT's induction entitlement (e.g. no cover; release time).

Each of these aspects will be discussed in detail, though as a brief overview, it was evident that the first of these - organising and/or convening a central programme of induction - ranked as a major activity for most of the secondary school induction coordinators; whilst, for reasons already outlined, it featured less in the sample of primary school induction managers. The equivalent activity in primary schools, with only one NQT to induct, would perhaps be undertaking individual interviews/tutorials. This role could also feature in the work of secondary school induction coordinators with responsibility for several NQTs. Most, but not all, primary and secondary school induction managers had involvement in observing/assessing NQTs. Only one-third of the coordinators in secondary schools reported working closely with their middle manager mentors.

The central induction programmes

- *Frequency and duration*

Each of the 12 case study secondary schools ran some form of central induction programme for its NQTs, offering a regular 'slot' for input and/or discussion. (One secondary school, with only a single NQT overseen by an induction manager with mentoring responsibilities also is included, because it conformed to the principle of specifically timetabling a regular period of NQT-focused support.). Three of the primary schools did likewise: in each case, a central programme was run by the headteacher. In one case, this was focused on the school's two NQTs, and in the two others, the programme ran for the school's contingent of NQT(s) **and** its other newly appointed staff.

Despite the prevalence of central induction programmes in secondary schools, there was considerable variation in the timing of these regular meetings. As Tables 4.4 and 4.5 show, major variations occurred not only as to **when** the programme ran, but for **how long** during the induction year. First, the timetabling of the programmes varied between schools:

Table 4.4: Timetabling of central induction sessions

Timing	Secondary	Primary
Lunch time	3	1
Lunchtime + after school	0	1
After school	7	1
During school time	2	0
Total	12	3

Thus, the majority of induction sessions were run after school and, where the length of session was ascertainable, were generally reported to last about an hour (or sometimes longer if the NQTs required it). In contrast, the lunchtime meetings were - with one notable exception - more typically described as taking up '20-30 minutes or so', with occasional concern expressed about the value of this particular slot.

> *The opportunity to have NQT central meetings should be out of school time - evenings (or even weekends) would be ideal ... it should be out of the school context - lunch times you can't open up with the next period looming.* (NQT: Secondary.)
>
> *NQT sessions run during the day would be a distraction from the job in hand.* (Induction coordinator: Secondary.)

Equally, NQTs and induction coordinators sometimes noted the difficulty of sustaining enthusiasm for long after-school sessions as the induction year got well underway (and other school commitments for the NQT emerged). One of the seven schools running an after-school programme used directed time to signal the importance of these sessions. Two schools used official NQT half-day release/non-contact time, interspersing school sessions with those run by the LEA. Despite these variations, it is important to stress that there were examples of central programmes in schools from each of the timetabling categories in Table 4.4 which received strong plaudits from the NQTs. A key factor seemed to be the existence of sufficient opportunity for ensuring the NQTs had confidence to express views and concerns. A central school programme that ran only short and/

or infrequent sessions - without other forums such as a residential or substantial summer induction put on by the school - might prohibit that solidarity:

The joint [monthly lunch time] meeting with the other NQTs is less valuable (than other parts of my induction), we don't actually have much solidarity. We are geographically dispersed in the school, and in the meetings, no-one else reveals their problems like me - even though you'd presume that NQTs in the same school would be close ... These meetings would only be useful if people opened up but in this case, they haven't.
(NQT: Secondary.)

The second issue, emerging in the above quote, is the frequency with which central induction sessions were held. Variation was not only evident in the weekly, fortnightly or monthly timing of these, but also whether the programme ran for one, two or three terms.

The three primary schools all held central induction meetings on a fortnightly basis, and two were sustained only through the first term, while the third continued until the end of the second term.

Table 4.5 shows the extent of the variation in the secondary school sample: plotting the frequency and duration of the twelve central programmes.

Table 4.5: *Frequency and duration of central induction sessions: secondary*

Frequency	Duration of sessions			
	No. of schools: Term 1 only	No. of schools: Terms 1 and 2	No. of schools: Terms 1, 2 and 3	Total
Monthly	1	2	1	4
Fortnightly	1	0	4	5
Weekly	0	0	3	3
Total	2	2	8	12

Several points emerge from this tabulated overview. First, and most obviously, the degree of variation testifies to considerable differences in the total amount of central support which the case study schools were providing for their NQTs. Second, the majority of the schools not only ran programmes throughout the year, but were more likely to do so when also providing frequent inputs (on a weekly or fortnightly basis). However, it must be added that several of the coordinators running such frequent and sustained programmes also indicated there was some reduction in the number of sessions towards the end of the year; that the programme finished in the middle of the third term, or that sessions were increasingly used for individual tutorials as well as group discussion. Nevertheless, overall it does suggest a fairly general recognition of the need to keep pace with the needs of NQTs throughout their first year, rather than front-load support to buttress only the early phase of an NQT's induction.

> *There is a danger of putting too much into just the first term, and letting it tail off in term 2 and term 3. In the first term, the NQT's prime concern is their teaching but in terms 2 and 3 when this is OK, they can be open to other school issues which they need to know about.*
> (Induction coordinator: Secondary.)

> *I think induction time should be found through the year because as an NQT, your needs change so much. Different things are required in term 1 so it's good to spread it over the year.* (NQT: Secondary.)

> *A down period for NQTs can occur and coincides with the twelve week point when as ITT students their teaching practice would finish, but as NQTs they realise the work is relentless till the end of the year. I'm adamant that support should be consistent throughout the year, and be particularly wary during that difficult second term.*
> (Induction coordinator: Secondary.)

As a concluding point, this sustained programme of support from most of the induction managers stands in notable contrast to the 'life-span' of many of the mentoring relationships (described in Chapter 6).

● *Content of central induction programmes: secondary*

This sub-section considers the subject or areas of concern which the sample of secondary school induction coordinators covered in their central sessions. It is important to stress that not all of them personally ran every session - sometimes other specialist staff (such as head of special needs or pastoral heads) were invited to lead or provide input. Indeed in one case, the school's deputy head with responsibility for induction ran no sessions at all herself, instead only organising the ten session programme. Notwithstanding this, Table 4.6 outlines, in alphabetical order, every topic covered by central sessions which were mentioned by the respondents in the course of the year's fieldwork programme, and also indicates in which term (1, 2 or 3) they were said to be covered. The data are taken from interviews and also from any documentation on the central programmes which the schools themselves produced.

Table 4.6: School induction programme: secondary

Term	Topics covered	Term	Topics covered
1	Able students	1; 2	Observation by NQT: procedures and feedback
3	Assertiveness (standing up to middle managers!)	1	Observation of NQT: procedures
1; 2	Assessment		
1; 2	Career development	1; 2	Parents: communication with/expectations
1; 3	Case-studies (of pupils)		
1; 2	Classroom management	1; 2; 3	Parents' evenings
1	Communication within the classroom	1; 2; 3	Pastoral support
		1	Pay and housing
2	Cross curricular themes	1	Philosophy of teaching
2; 3	Cross phase links/ the new intake	1; 2	Profiling
		1; 3	Professionalism
1; 2	Differentiation	2	PSHE
	Difficult children	2	Pupil centred learning
1; 2; 3	Discipline	1; 2; 3	Pupil pursuit
1; 2	Equal opportunities	1	Recording and reporting
1; 3	Examinations	1	Record keeping
2	Extra curriculum activities	1; 2	Records of achievement
3	External agencies	1	Resource management
3	Finance	3	Review of induction programme (year)
3	Flexible learning		
1; 2; 3	Form tutor role	1	Review of induction programme (term)
1; 2	Governors; roles and expectations		
		2	School management (senior roles)
3	Health and safety		
1	Hidden curriculum/ Ethos of the school	1; 2; 3	Special needs
		1	The staff handbook: questions answered
1; 2	Information technology		
2	Key Stage 4	1; 2	Time/stress management
1; 2	Lesson planning	1	Use of NQT's profile
1	The local community of the school	1	Welcome lunch/evening
2	Managing children's behaviour	3	The whole curriculum/ timetabling
2	Managing marking		
1	Meeting recent NQTs	1	Work experience

The list can be categorised into various themes (or, as one induction coordinator called them *'the body of professional issues all NQTs should consider'*), showing the range of input which the sample of secondary NQTs received. However, with the variation in frequency and duration of school central induction already outlined, inevitably not all NQTs received full coverage of each of these 'themes'.

The main themes which emerge from Table 4.6 are:

- **pupil learning** e.g. able students; differentiation; special needs
- **teaching strategies** e.g. classroom management; discipline; flexible learning approaches
- **the administration of learning** e.g. parents reports; recording and record keeping
- **pastoral roles** e.g. PSHE; form tutoring
- **the school context** e.g. local community; governors; cross phase links; school management
- **the wider curriculum** e.g. cross curriculum links; IT (across the curriculum)
- **NQT needs** e.g. time/stress management; career development
- **induction issues** e.g. use of profile; observation procedures; progress review of programme; welcome lunch/evening

Coverage of these themes could also vary in approach. Some programmes included structured first-hand opportunities for observation by the NQTs to address such issues as teaching strategies, pupil learning (e.g. pupil pursuits/ tracking), and others encouraged visits to feeder primaries; work with the special needs department, etc.

Beyond that, some induction coordinators were said to operate with extreme skill in leading group discussion, offering, in effect, sophisticated adult learning strategies for encouraging reflective discourse and for building rapport and trust between the NQTs. Where induction coordinators received most acclaim from their NQTs, there was always evidence of coordinator commitment to the induction process, but, often, as well, an identifiable rationale or value-system underpinning it.

> *NQTs have an attitude which it is worth the school using and not dampening - a certain freshness, optimism, enthusiasm and lack of cynicism. A good school should realise teachers teach in different ways and have different strengths. Our deputy (i/c induction) has been strongly involved with us, and it's good to have that support from on high, have that link. It's nice to know she - and therefore SMT - value*

NQTs and what they can give. It [all] depends on the ethos - they have the ethos which understands people's differences and strengths.
(NQT: Secondary.)

Reflexivity is a long term aim of SMT and a key part of the induction programme. Once you are a reflective practitioner you never let it go. Reflective practitioners have better stress levels, they see the classroom as a set of inter-connected events, they are part of it, they can manipulate events and do it for professional reasons - that removes the emotion from the situation ... It's important the school allows people to say what is going wrong - that's a school ethos. NQTs, like all teachers, must be encouraged to identify what's wrong and how to solve it.
(DH i/c induction: Secondary.)

NQTs come to school with a range of skills and there is a need to build on those. In a sense the profile helps because it acknowledges these skills and starts from wherever the NQTs are. I have identified certain areas to include in the induction programme, but it is also very flexible and, above all, I encourage NQT **participation**. *In a sense, I see it as a bit like a group therapy session - how can we, as a group, support individuals. The programme is totally negotiable, and I will discuss with the NQTs where it should go next term.* (DH i/c induction: Secondary.)

- *Central induction programmes: primary*

Though only three of the 18 primary schools ran a direct equivalent of the secondary induction programmes, in a small number of the other primaries there was evidence of a trend to structure and organise input from colleagues – such as subject curriculum coordinators, assessment and special needs specialists to help the development of the school's NQT(s).

Examples included:

- one-to-one discussion on policies/schemes of work in mutual non-contact time between NQTs and the school's subject coordinators in turn
- opportunities for the NQT to observe subject coordinators, and to be observed by them

These were sometimes constructed into a series of inputs, and hence could be said to constitute a programme. However, such inputs did not have the frequency of the majority of the secondary programmes.

Individual sessions with the induction manager

Some secondary school coordinators also made reference to undertaking individual tutorials with NQTs as a component of the central induction programme. This role for induction managers was also very evident in the primary school sample, with its typical single NQT appointee, and often appeared as the nearest equivalent to the secondary school induction managers' central programmes. A number of primary school induction managers, especially those who did not combine the role with mentoring, recounted how they might, periodically, set aside time for a one-to-one discussion with their NQT.

At the end of each half-term, the NQT talks with me about problems and successes, and where she might want support in the future. The discussion also identifies a focus for practice for the next half term, and also the NQT's ideas for her own professional development beyond induction. I will then organise for that. Also I think NQTs bring a new dimension to the staff, a freshness and can see things which established staff can't. So, the professional development discussion will include the NQT's ideas for development in the school. (Headteacher: Primary.)

[We meet to discuss] a termly report from me, which I want the NQT to contribute to because critical appraisal of oneself is a key characteristic for professional development. As well as that, there is a meeting per half term, minimum, between me and the NQT, which forms part of assessment and observation, includes choosing a focus for development.
(Headteacher: Primary.)

It was evident that, in both the primary and secondary schools, these individual sessions usually had a specific focus relating to assessment/observation, e.g. a termly review of progress; providing post-observation feedback, and perhaps also beforehand clarifying the procedures or negotiating a focus for observation. Other induction managers recounted undertaking individual interviews on career development:

At the end of the year, I will spend an hour with each NQT reviewing their year and their futures. In truth, some NQTs at this stage barely tolerate what they see as interference, whereas others are already thinking about future career moves and very much welcome this interest in their development. It is a different, but important aspect of my role to help NQTs consider career development. (DH i/c induction: Secondary.)

The head, who also has a significant role in induction, has recently completed an appraisal interview with the NQT. The NQT was worried that he'd ask her deep searching questions about her professionalism. I think he did but she came out of it very well and was very pleased. The head also thanked her for all her work - he's very good at these interviews and tries to map out what the NQT or teacher has done and where they see themselves going. (Mentor: Primary.)

Although induction managers in both the primary and secondary case study schools implemented this particular aspect of the role, it was also clear that, overall, the sample of primary school NQTs received formalised input from their induction managers very much less frequently than their secondary counterparts; the 'themes' covered did not entirely match those identified in the secondary school central programmes. Those most evident in the individual sessions of primary school induction managers included:

- **the administration of learning** e.g. planning; recording procedures; schemes of work; reporting to parents
- **induction issues** e.g. progress review; foci for development; feedback on observation
- **NQT needs:** e.g. career/professional development

Thus, such themes as **pupil learning**; and **teaching strategies** did not appear to feature directly in the repertoire (or input) of primary school induction managers unless perhaps they also had an official mentoring role. However, the primary school induction managers' use of individual tutorial sessions sometimes had an element which was only rarely apparent in those of their secondary counterparts: namely, the negotiation of individual programmes of development and appropriate use of non-contact entitlements. From an individual termly or half-termly session, these primary school induction managers might arrange for NQTs to spend time with other colleagues (particularly subject coordinators), or organise visits to other schools in order to provide support on particular needs (such as an unfamiliar National Curriculum subject, special needs, assessment, differentiation).

The NQT has continued her half-day out of the classroom, determining her own programme within that time. It's trying all the time to make her responsible for the kinds of things she wants to see. We discussed her focus and I have facilitated her visit to see good evidence of differentiation. I located the school where good practice in differentiation was reported after she selected the focus. (Headteacher: Primary.)

Finally, exclusive to the primary school sample was the view that induction managers could and should play a low key and non-participatory role in their NQT's induction, though this invariably occurred where the school's mentoring arrangements were seen to be particularly strong and effective:

I will observe the NQT at the end of term, and we'll have a discussion afterwards. But otherwise it's my policy to keep a low profile, though I do monitor by going in the classroom, discussing informally with the NQT and mentor. This is a deliberate attempt to maintain the possibility of dialogue with the NQT, rather than induction being seen as a threatening kind of judgement. (Headteacher: Primary.)

I want to stay in the background. I can't afford to be so involved with the NQT; there are times I need to be distant from it. I much prefer to stay supporting from the sidelines - you can't be a friend and confidante one minute and the next minute being the head and saying 'this is wrong'. An active and directive role in induction by me might be necessary if there are serious problems. (Headteacher: Primary.)

CHAPTER 5
SCHOOL INDUCTION: ASSESSMENT AND ENTITLEMENTS

This chapter continues to focus on the role of the school in the induction process. It does this by examining the observation of NQTs for assessment purposes and the training of mentors in schools for this and other functions. It also considers the important role that induction managers play in administering NQTs' rights and entitlements.

Observation for assessment

A further major role for most (but not all) induction managers in the case study schools was that of observing the NQTs as part of an assessment of their progress. Table 5.1 shows the variation in how often those with responsibility for induction in the school undertook formal observations.

Table 5.1: Occasion of formal observations by induction managers

	None	One term only	Term 1+2	Term 1+3	Term 1+2+3
Secondary	2	3	3	3	1
Primary	4	6	3	3	2

Thus, only a very small number of either the primary or secondary school induction managers undertook formal observations in each term. Of those observing only in one term, all six primary school induction managers said they observed in the first term, whilst the three secondary school coordinators each observed in different terms. LEA advisory staffs' or mentors' observations were often evident in the other terms.

Accounts of the type of observation undertaken by induction managers (and equally middle managers/mentors) ranged from the formal - with agreed procedures and protocols - to, especially in primary, the very informal - a common phraseology being 'I pop in now and then/a lot'. This range of observation procedures is illustrated in the following comments:

> *Of central concern this [first] term has been the assessment or lesson observation, and the preparation for this. I've given notes on this to all the HoDs on the preliminary meeting, observation and debriefing. I'm doing my observations on the staff development/appraisal model. Beforehand, I show each NQT the LEA assessment forms and my comments and we go over them. During the lesson observations, I will scribble down more notes so we have evidence on which to base out discussions/debriefing. The HoD or departmental mentor will also be expected to observe [in this way].* (Induction coordinator: Secondary.)

> *...[the mentor has not observed] and any observation by me over the year has been informal - I've looked in the classroom during the evening, looked at her planning, checked children's books. The NQT's been observed casually as her children move round school, do PE. There are people in her classroom a lot - I know she is succeeding.*
> (Headteacher: Primary.)

> *NQT assessment, by the LEA and by me, is increasingly going into an appraisal model, agreeing a focus for observation and knowing the time of the visit. Both the mentor and I observe, but only my observations will feed into the adviser's comments and assessment (if the mentor's comments did, it would break down that special relationship). Before half-term in the first term, my observations were based on questions which the NQT herself wanted to know about her practice, and were formulated together in discussion. These formed the basis of a discussion afterwards ... I also observe at the end of each term, at two different times of the day, and again there'll be discussion after that.* (Headteacher: Primary.)

> *I have done a formal observation of the NQT this term, but she was not aware of it. I thought the children were well motivated and keen. I took the opportunity to look at books and pick up on one or two things that the NQT needed to address. I think it was useful for the NQT - it made her think about her practice.* (Mentor: Secondary.)

Such variation in both the kind and amount of observation which an NQT might receive may be a cause for concern, as might the variation in how many observers were forming a judgement of NQTs' teaching.

Table 5.2 offers an overview of who, within the school staff, undertook any formal observation of the NQT sample during their induction year, and includes a category of 'none/informal' where schools indicated that, throughout the year, no official occasion for observation was instituted.

TABLE 5.2: School personnel undertaking observation of NQTs

	Secondary N =12	Primary N=18
Induction manager only	0	4
Induction manager/mentor only	0	3
Induction manager/mentor + Head	2	2
Induction manager + mentor	8	3
Mentor only	2	2
None/informal	0	4
Total	12	18

The table reveals a number of issues. First, all the NQTs in secondary schools had formalised observations by school personnel, whereas four of the primary school NQTs had none. This absence generally occurred when their mentor had full time classroom commitment; when the induction manager stressed that lack of formal observation was partly due to the capability of the NQT, and that they had used informal methods for ascertaining that classroom capability. Primary school induction managers often pointed out that in the formative assessment of their NQT, they utilised many 'clues' or 'cues' ascertained from 'passing through' the NQT's teaching space in open plan buildings; from taking over the class in NQT's absence, accompanying NQTs on outdoor trips and so on. However, one headteacher acknowledged this may omit an important potential developmental function of formal observation:

> *I haven't observed on a formal basis this term, I've only popped in. It's not been necessary because of her ability. But things like the right manner for* ***them*** *with the children (which is very personal and innate), and the individual teacher's routines do need looking at: standing back and observing might be a more useful way to appraise and improve that for the NQT.* (Headteacher: Primary.)

A second point to emerge from Table 5.2 is the number of NQTs who have only a single observer looking at their practice. Again, there was a noticeable difference between the primary and secondary school samples.

In only two secondary schools did the induction coordinator/manager not observe the NQT(s), and in each of these examples, an external observer in the form of an LEA adviser or inspector undertook a classroom visit as well as the HoD/mentor. In one of the schools, the induction coordinator instead took part in a three-way termly review with the adviser and NQT in the light of the latter's observation. In the ten other case study secondary schools,

NQTs were observed for assessment purposes by both mentor and senior manager (induction coordinator and/or headteacher). Hence, no secondary NQT was 'judged' by only one 'classroom assessor'.

In contrast, nine of the primary school NQTs had only one observer from the school, and four of those had no adviser visit supplementing school observations. As well as that, three of the primary NQTs who had no official/formal observations undertaken by school induction managers or mentors also had no adviser visit. Thus, altogether, seven of the 20 primary NQTs were without a second opinion on their teaching.

Perhaps, not surprisingly, some of the primary NQTs voiced uncertainty about if or how there was assessment of them and, equally significantly, expressed some disappointment that there was no formal feedback on their teaching.

I haven't really had any feedback on my performance and that is something which I feel would be really useful. It would be helpful to have someone say that perhaps you could try this, or this is working well. This is what happened during TP and although it's not particularly nice to be observed, it is beneficial for someone to give you feedback. I think it would be helpful to introduce something like that in the future. It's not an open plan class and I don't have a shared area, so if I close my door, then no one really knows what I'm doing. You do need some feedback to reassure you that you're doing OK. Am I in fact doing it the same as other teachers in the school. (NQT: Primary.)

I've had no formal observation or written report on a lesson. I get feedback from my mentor, but I've never had a written record. I think that would've been helpful. I would have welcomed more formal observation and feedback. (NQT: Primary.)

Coming from industry into teaching, I'm used to being appraised six monthly, and I've specifically had to ask for as assessment from either the mentor or deputy (i/c induction) or head. I've asked for a report on me, where they think I've done well and where there's room for improvement. The more critical the better for me, I don't want a whitewash. (NQT: Primary.)

In contrast, all the secondary school NQTs could recount examples of formal observation by senior staff or middle manager mentors which were seen as helpful, reassuring, etc. and this seemed especially the case where profiles/competences or agreed foci were part of the procedures. Equally, there were plenty of examples where middle managers were said to 'pop in' to NQTs lessons, in much the same way as described in the primary school sample.

A major problem voiced in secondary schools was that of organising the time for sustained observation and for substantial feedback by both senior and middle management staff. Indeed, one induction coordinator calculated that each of her six NQTs had been given 'at least three hours' of her time in the final term's round of pre-observation discussion, observation, and feedback. Whilst most induction managers could find time for their observation/assessment role, it was middle managers who had most problems:

Observation is an expectation of my job as deputy head. Middle managers are finding it more difficult to find time for observation, especially when their 'free' periods don't coincide with the NQTs. Resourcing and time for observation is a problem, a burden for them - it's not only observation but setting up the observation (which competences from the profile to look at) and the feedback. It's an issue we need to address. (Induction coordinator: Secondary.)

I have so much else to do, but I know I ought to have more time to observe my NQT. I hate penalising my own pupils in order to observe ... there ought to be more flexibility in the mentor's timetable to be able to go in and watch. Due recognition for induction should be given by giving all HoDs with NQTs and extra free period. (HoD: Secondary.)

The problem of the availability of time and human resources may also account for the shortage of observation in so many of the primary school sample.

Despite these difficulties, it is important to stress that all the schools gave detailed accounts of how NQTs experiencing problems would be given greater attention, including, in some instances, the invitation for LEA personnel to observe and contribute an opinion. It was clear that such problems would not pass unnoticed nor unsupported. (Chapter 9 provides further details of the LEA's role in this and related areas.)

Finally, though several induction managers were adamant that schools' increasing responsibility for NQTs was appropriate and preferable to the old LEA observation/assessment procedures, others raised concerns about the implications.

It was important to have the individual adviser coming into school. If it was other senior colleagues from other schools who were called on to perform the outside-judgement role, the NQT might rightly say 'who are they?' Advisers had the assurance of a certain professional neutrality. It will need a meeting between me, the outside judge and the NQT to clarify the ground rules. (Induction coordinator: Secondary.)

It will be very difficult, without external LEA support to make a judgement on the NQT which will affect a future career. Pitching that judgement is

a real problem especially if you haven't had an NQT for some time. I'm afraid the easy answer will be the one year contract.
(Headteacher: Primary.)

As well as these contractual issues raised by schools' increasing assessment responsibility for NQTs, the demise of outside LEA assessment/observation was also noted to have professional development implications:

An LEA adviser feels the need to mention certain things because they're educational issues; a teacher with a busy day who is observing you might mention basic things which they think are important as they see it, and not take it to quite the same level as an adviser with time to sit back and who has distance from the job. Both have positive aspects but there's more subtlety perhaps in the LEA comments, the school's [comments after observation] tend to be straightforward, to the point 'I'd do that, that and may be think about these things - but only ... is a realistic expectation'. Compared to that, the LEA adviser can bring in bigger issues, ideas and ideals. (NQT: Secondary.)

Putting together all the evidence from the case studies, it suggests that schools as yet may not always have the time, resources or even intent to undertake termly analytical assessment of their NQTs' classroom performance. Consistency between schools in their observation procedures was not at all apparent.

Schools' mentor training

Given the increasing responsibility of schools for induction and assessment of their NQTs, several secondary school induction coordinators raised the key issue of the need for consistency between middle managers in the way they carried out assessment or mentoring responsibilities generally. Ensuring equivalence within the institution was both an administrative task for induction managers and also, crucially, one requiring some sort of training programme for those designated as mentors.

There need to be a formal link between mentors, more consistency between them, now that they increasingly replace the LEA role. It has to be a formality that will stand up against any dissatisfaction from an NQT that they've had a raw deal. (Induction coordinator: Secondary.)

Senior management must express its commitment to the investment in NQTs. We need a school policy which lays down what is expected involved in induction. We have a staff development need in both mentoring and observation. That needs to go into the School Development Plan. (Induction coordinator: Secondary.)

In the sample of 12 secondary schools, only two induction coordinators had already instituted formal 'training' for their middle manager mentors (both, significantly, were instituting competence-based profiles for mentor/NQT use). One induction coordinator had regular meetings of mentors to air issues and concerns (this was described as information transmission rather than training, and significantly, not all mentors always attended). Another induction coordinator referred to her written communication with the department heads regarding assessment and observation procedures as well as informal one-to-one communication (staff-room conversations). Thus, in eight of the 12 schools, it was apparent that there were very few or no procedures/mechanisms for induction coordinators to engage with the school's middle managers or designated mentors. This omission was sometimes noted by mentors themselves, who often also pinpointed a lack of coordination between their work as mentors and the induction coordinator's activity:

> *I do feel that induction here is not fully integrated into a total programme. Departmental support does not complement the [induction manager's] programme. I know nothing of what goes on in those sessions. I asked if I needed a checklist of things that I should cover from term 1 to term 3 - there really is a need for much more of a [total] training programme for NQTs. At the moment it's very ad hoc and reactive.*
>
> (HoD/mentor: Secondary.)

> *If a school induction programme is deemed valuable, mentors should be more involved in it, on a far more formal basis than now. Faculty heads could and should make a contribution to induction more generally and formally. Our involvement should be timetabled. I'd [also] like some sessions on the assessment of NQTs with the other HoFs, to go through it together and achieve a common approach.* (HoF/mentor: Secondary.)

The training of secondary middle managers for their role in induction thus seemed one of the major outstanding needs, largely unfulfilled at either school or LEA level.

Administering NQT entitlements

Induction managers often defined an important aspect of their role as 'protecting' the NQTs, or 'guaranteeing' entitlements.

> *You've got to have someone in the SMT who will fight for them and stand ground, you've got to shield them from HoFs giving them the worst classes and so on. ... The key issue in the management of induction is that against all the pressures coming on schools and all the changes, uncertainty [you have to] keep [their entitlement] stable and keep it*

*protected. NQTs are our future, and in keeping their entitlement safe, we produce people who want to teach and continue to be enthusiastic. Whatever the financial pressures or cynicism around, we have to keep **an oasis in the middle** and say even though these special protected conditions won't always be like this for them, it's how we produce the best people we can.* (Induction coordinator: Secondary.)

Since September, our NQT has been guaranteed - and that's a strange word to be using in education - a half day a week release. It fell down only when we had staff absence, other than that it's been fully protected.
(Headteacher: Primary.)

Many respondents recognised the special case of NQTs and the need to ensure some form of decreased workload, or occasion for developmental activity. Again, in this area, the variation between primary and secondary school induction provision was evident: perhaps partly because the generalist class teacher role and staff deployment in primary schools is inherently less flexible than the timetabled subject specialist plus the (possible) form tutoring commitment of the secondary practitioner.

Hence, secondary NQTs' main types of decreased workload could include guarantees of no cover, no form tutor roles, and a reduced timetable. In primary schools, a regular reduced teaching commitment was not evident in over half the sample, and any decreased workload (apart from attending LEA induction sessions) often consisted of the provision of extra classroom support or occasional release for observation. Each of these strategies for supporting the NQT will be discussed in turn.

- *reduced timetable*

In the primary sample, a total of seven schools offered their NQT(s) a guaranteed weekly half-day release. Six of these were from two London boroughs, where this entitlement was a traditional component of LEA induction, with the half-day being used for LEA induction sessions as well as non-contact time at school. Only one other primary school induction manager, from a metropolitan borough, **chose** to sustain the same entitlement for their NQT. Another provided half-day release, by the headteacher/mentor covering, every three to four weeks to allow the NQT to visit other schools. A third primary school offered cover by the head on a once a half-termly basis to undertake observation in the school, and in one other school, cover for the NQT to undertake weekly one hour observations in the first term was reported. For the rest, (i.e. eight schools) any non-contact time was the equivalent of that offered to the rest of the staff, though it was often used in ways which directly supported induction, e.g. observation within or at another school, discussion with coordinators, etc.

In the secondary school sample, nine of the twelve schools gave their NQTs extra non-contact time. Three specified a half-day per week entitlement (again all in London boroughs) and six specified the non-contact time was one or more periods lighter than for main grade or standard scale teachers. In terms of actual amount of time, this could vary from 45 to 150 minutes per week.

Clearly, the timetabling arrangements for secondary NQTs needed to be planned in advance, and late appointments may prove problematic. Providing primary NQTs with weekly reduced timetables was far less possible given typical staffing arrangements in the primary sector: some schools even suggested it would be detrimental to pupil-teacher relationships. Nevertheless, the marked discrepancy between primary and secondary NQTs' rights or entitlement to non-contact or release time may be a cause for concern. For some it represents another example of the non-equivalence evident in so many aspects of resourcing for the two sectors. A number of primary NQTs referred to the 'ideal' of having extra time to plan, appraise and evaluate their practice during the initial part of their induction year particularly: *'more release in the first term would have been helpful, just time to prepare and organise your own class'*.

- *opportunities for observation*

The ways in which NQTs made use of any extra release or non-contact time, varied considerably. Some NQTs stressed the need to utilise the additional time to mark, prepare and record, whereas others undertook, as well, observations within or beyond the school or stipulated it was being used to evaluate and review practice. In other words, there was a key difference in perceptions as to whether decreasing the workload of an NQT was predominantly an **amelioration** strategy or a **development** opportunity. Overall, primary NQTs' explanations of their use of non-contact time seemed to suggest that they saw such release as an opportunity for developmental activity rather more often than their secondary school colleagues. In five of the 12 secondary schools, the NQTs stated they had not undertaken observations: in contrast, only three of the 18 primary schools did not ensure some opportunity for observation:

> *[This first term], I have one hour non-contact on Wednesday afternoon to observe other classes, other teachers, and if I want a visit to other schools it can be arranged. My major and initial concern was classroom control - I wanted to see other age-groups in the school and colleagues and the sorts of children being taught. I was watching how teachers were using voice control, how they used positive teaching, such as pupil contracts.* (NQT: Primary.)

> *[Like the other teachers here], my non-contact time is for record-keeping and assessment. But I used it for the first half-term to observe in classrooms, to work out where I fitted in, what else was going on in the school. I talked to siblings, looked at what the teacher did in the classroom, their techniques and also children's levels of work. It was first-hand familiarisation.* (NQT: Primary.)

It is important to stress that some secondary school induction managers (and mentors) did institute very structured observation opportunities within their central programmes, such as a full day of pupil tracking, visits to other schools' subject departments, and even, in one case, the opportunity for the NQTs to return to their training institution for updates on subject specialism. Others were also beginning to recognise the need to formalise observation within the induction programme:

> *Observation is a good idea and just trying to impress on NQTs the importance or availability of observation is not good enough on its own. It must be timetabled and programmed because observation is not their top priority, it's preparing the next lesson, marking and so on.*
> (HoD: Secondary.)

Observation opportunities were universally highly valued by NQTs, and the importance of observing others was often stressed by induction managers and mentors. The main difference of opinion was whether observation in other institutions had great value in the first year of induction, with particularly some primary school induction managers stressing the need for NQTs to avoid the insularity of one institution. Others felt strongly that an understanding and absorption of their own school's approaches was a first priority before encountering that of others.

Notwithstanding this, the principle of structured and focused observation opportunities may rank as an area which schools' induction programmes increasingly should address as they take on board developmental responsibilities. Moreover, NQTs could testify to its value throughout their induction year, selecting foci which matched their changing concerns.

- *cover arrangements and form tutoring*

Two areas of decreased workload, exclusive to secondary schools, were whether NQTs should undertake cover duties and form tutoring responsibility. Different rationales underpinning relief from cover and form tutoring responsibilities were put forward: sometimes the emphasis was to ensure and guarantee a lighter workload and sometimes to spare NQTs from particularly 'threatening' teaching situations.

Clearly, some 'cost' implications were involved in employing staff who were then alleviated of these responsibilities, and schools varied as to how far they thought it was both possible and preferable for their NQTs not to take on these typical secondary practitioner duties. Some induction managers argued strongly that the lower salary costs of NQTs could be offset by the recognition that these arduous and demanding duties should not be asked of inexperienced newcomers. Others saw it as a necessary part of NQTs' learning.

> *We try and keep the first term as a learning and fitting in term. In the first term, non-contact time is sacrosanct, they do not have a form tutor role. However, with seven NQTs it does become difficult to protect no cover if the school is then required to buy in supply cover and the budget is spent up. So, later in the year, some able NQTs will be used. But a lot of protection must go on into the first term and that's possible if a deputy head is in charge of induction.* (Induction coordinator: Secondary.)

> *With extra non-contact time, no cover as sacrosanct, shared school duties and co-form tutoring (as well as quality time from senior and middle managers), it costs the school a lot more to take on an NQT on a low incremental point instead of an experienced teacher. ... NQTs are an investment into which a fair whack of valuable resources have to be put.* (Induction coordinator: Secondary.)

Given this range of attitudes, the secondary school sample offered a number of different approaches to NQTs and cover duties. These were:

- no cover: 'sacrosanct'/protected throughout the year (as far as possible)
- no cover for the first term
- immediate inclusion in cover timetable if the NQT was deemed 'suitable'.

Approaches to form-tutoring showed the following variations:

- no form tutoring until second year of teaching
- shadow tutoring/co-tutoring
- optional after the first term
- immediate full responsibility for a form

Form tutoring was mentioned by some NQTs as a particular issue, as one put it: ' *.. it creates so much work, it's quite stressful, and very very time-consuming'*. There were examples of NQTs wishing to take up this responsibility at the earliest opportunity and others suggesting it was inappropriate to do so. Some pointed out how unprepared they were for form-tutoring by their initial training. The consensus of best practice - from induction managers, mentors and NQTs - was very much that there should be a gradual introduction into this aspect of the secondary practitioner's role:

I think it would've been better not to give me a form, especially in my first term. All the pupils except for Y7 are not new to the school and are streetwise - they try to pull one over you. That's not pleasant. I'd recommend working alongside an experienced form tutor, ideally for a whole year, at least for the first term. (NQT: Secondary.)

It's a good thing to keep NQTs away from form tutoring if you can or at least get them to act as a deputy form-tutor. From my experience I've found the one grey area where NQTs are least prepared is for form tutor work. If you wanted to be effective you would not put your NQTs straight into form tutor work. ... Ideally it would be best to team up an NQT with an experienced tutor to go through the first year and gradually take over. (HoY: Secondary.)

This comment suggests a need for some kind of mentoring or modelling in form tutoring and yet - as the next chapter will show - the role of mentor is one where schools' time and resources could not always match intentions and ideals. Nevertheless, the value of investing in training in this area was spelt out by the pastoral head quoted above:

I think initial training should be looking at PSE much more than they currently do, partly because a lot of learning and counselling techniques you learn can be applied generally to your teaching. (HoY: Secondary.)

- *subject coordination*

As far as primary schools were concerned, it was generally the case that NQTs were not asked to take on the role of subject or curriculum coordinator in their first year. Only five of the primary NQTs were asked to perform this role during induction (and one of these was only from term three onwards). In all cases the subject areas were either art or physical education. Several NQTs had asked to take on the role but headteachers were very conscious of 'the state of readiness' of the new teacher before either agreeing to such requests or suggesting they might wish to take on a subject responsibility. However, there were expectations - usually by both senior managers and NQTs themselves - that such a curriculum leadership role would be embraced in year two.

The following four examples or 'cameos' of actual school induction programmes provide a summary of how schools support their NQTs. In terms of the models of induction support outlined in Chapter 2, cameos 1, 2, and 4 are examples of multi-support systems as there is evidence of coordination between the various levels, whereas cameo 3 is an example of a bi-support system.

School induction programmes: four cameos

Cameo One

School: 11-16   1086 pupils   72 staff   7 NQTs
Induction Manager: DH i/c staff development (8 yrs i/c induction)
Mentor: Second in department

Summer period:
On appointment, arrangements were made between HoD and NQT to spend several days in the department: one HoD was reported to have invited their NQT to the department's weekend INSET.

Central programme:
A fortnightly lunch-time meeting throughout three terms. In term one, new teachers also were expected to attend, thereafter the programme was optional for them. This school's programme also included a weekend residential for NQTs and new teachers ('at a nice peaceful hotel'), in the latter part of the first term, which had a strong focus on personal/stress management and equal opportunities.

Themes in the lunch-time sessions included:

Term 1: mixed ability teaching/differentiation; special needs; approaching parents; report writing; case studies of handling classroom problems

Term 2: a non-contact day for classroom observation (including pre- and de-briefing); marking; parent's evenings

Term 3: video material analysis, review/evaluation of the year's programme

Individual interviews/assessment:
The induction manager held termly individual review meetings with NQT and LEA subject advisor or NQT's HoD, to discuss progress.

Observation for assessment:
This was the responsibility of the mentor.

Mentor training:
'At least three meetings a year' between mentors and DH were stipulated in school's induction policy statement. Topics included report writing, how to offer constructive and positive feedback.

NQT entitlements:
No cover in term one; no form-tutoring until year 2; extra non-contact.

Comment:
An induction programme with a strong commitment to reflection, analysis of classroom interaction as a way of empowering the teacher. The protection of NQTs from cover and form tutoring was stressed. The case study NQT expressed great approval of her school induction and also her induction manager:

> *[our induction manager] is so highly organised, and her enthusiasm as a teacher bounces onto you, she has had a marvellous impact on everybody. She's made us very confident and sure of ourselves, she's dedicated to her job, her enthusiasm is imparted onto you and it makes you better in the classroom, it carries through.*

Cameo Two

School: 12-16 580 pupils 40 staff 4 NQTs
Induction manager: DH i/c ITT and induction (2.5 yrs i/c induction)
Mentor: HoD

Summer period:
Two days unpaid, the majority of time spent with HoD, receiving schemes of work, timetable, staff handbook.

Central programme:
Fortnightly meetings after school, with first term programme also for all new staff. Content and timing were increasingly responsive to NQT needs: it was the consensus NQT opinion that the programme should continue for the year but decrease to meetings every three weeks during the second term.

Themes included:

Term 1: Special needs; parents; classroom management; the NQT profile; NQTs undertaking 'case studies/research' into difficult pupils

Term 2: RoA, time management - planning and marking; pair/group discussion of a compilation of classic classroom problem situations

Term 3: career plans; prioritising; difficult children; learning to say no to MMs

Individual interviews:
Undertaken during the year, based on a profile.

Observation for assessment:
The induction manager observed in the second and third terms. The HoDs' observations utilised the profile.

Mentor training:
Training for middle managers in the use of the profile was undertaken at school by the LEA induction advisory teacher. The induction manager also ran sessions during the year, and worked individually with the mentors. Issues covered also included observation skills.

NQT entitlements:
One extra free period; no form tutor role, though NQTs encouraged to 'shadow' a form, and gradually take over its running through the year. This involved attending all tutor and PSE sessions, thus giving the NQTs 'status in the eyes of pupils'.

Comment:
A strong focus on the NQTs own agenda after term one was apparent, with strategies to encourage discussion of classroom difficulties. The school's commitment to the induction profile involved the induction manager having extended individual discussion with mentor as well as training sessions. The NQT said of her induction programme:

It's been very very helpful and supportive. It's always been flexible and right from the outset we've made up our own agenda about what we think is crucial. We can socialise as well. It's a nice way to unburden yourself, all the meetings have proved extremely useful. They've helped break down isolation and provided a forum for us.

Cameo Three

School: 4-11   232 pupils   9 (FTE) staff   1 NQT
Induction manager: Headteacher
Mentor: B allowance, adjacent teaching area and age group

Summer period:
The NQT came into school for three weeks unpaid, working with the teacher of the age range she was to take and the children who would be in her class the following September, as well as spending time on looking at year plans.

Central programme/individual interviews:
The headteacher went over NQT's planning in depth at the start of the year, and in term 3 had extended discussion on the NQT's coordinator role.

During the induction year, each of the school's subject coordinators spent mutual non-contact time with the NQT going over the policy and schemes of work for their particular curriculum area.

Observation for assessment:
The induction manager/headteacher undertook observation each term, and also observed informally throughout the year. The mentor observed once 'to fulfil the LEA requirements'.

Mentor training:
Undertaken by the LEA.

NQT entitlement:
No extra release specified.

Comment:
This school exemplified a particularly systematic deployment of school subject expertise to contribute to the NQT's induction. The placement of the NQT next to her mentor was also a deliberate strategy. Of the impact of the school induction, the NQT stated:

> *I find it very useful to be in post, on the job and asking people and getting support. The ideas that are suggested formally or informally - in staff room talk as well as talking more formally with the coordinators, I'll go away and try those. I've had a go at what's been suggested, I've used the advice and made it my own, done it my way, rather than just copying it.*

She added that a possible improvement would be to have the opportunity to observe her coordinator colleagues teaching their subject expertise.

Cameo Four

School: 7-11 500 pupils 20 staff 1 NQT (& 2 new teachers)
Induction manager: DH non-class based (8 yrs i/c induction)
Mentor: (i) DH and (ii) year group leader

Summer period:
The NQT was given accommodation by a staff member and expenses were paid for a week's presence in school. The time was spent planning with the year group where the NQT was to teach; involvement in a staff INSET day; and working with the class she was to teach. A purely social occasion also was set up: the NQT was taken out for a meal by staff.

Central programme:
A fortnightly lunch time meeting in the first term was run by the headteacher for the NQT and two other new staff. The DH also attended these meetings. It covered such issues as the role of governors and school trips. The NQT also participated in weekly meetings of the year group which the headteacher might also attend. The NQT was encouraged to join a school working party in her subject specialism.

Individual interviews:
The headteacher held an extensive annual professional development interview with each staff member, including the NQT. There was also on-going one-to one discussions with each mentor.

Observation for assessment:
The head observed formally in term one, and at the same time there were informal visits and extensive classroom support from the DH/mentor and year group leader.

Mentor training:
The DH/mentor had, in the past, provided input to termly LEA mentor meetings which had now ceased.

NQT entitlements:
No extra release but considerable extra classroom support from DH/mentor, especially in term one; opportunity for observation within the school: (the school managers did not see any benefit in visits to other schools during the first year of teaching.)

Comment:
This school illustrated a highly structured induction programme, with clear written guidelines and a formal checklist delineating the particular contribution of head, DH and year group leader. (Dates of coverage of the various issues in the checklist were also to be completed.) The thoroughness of support was very apparent, and the NQT could pinpoint that it had strongly influenced her practice. Of its impact she stated:

My meetings with [the DH/mentor] and [year group leader], and the mentor visits [to my classroom] are all affecting the way I think and my practice. The support I've had has enabled me to look at how I'm doing things and ways in which it might be improved. It's difficult to pinpoint any one thing. I think my teaching style has changed - it's become more integrated: I don't think I could've coped with that as a student (with different children doing different things at different times of the day). I feel confident now ... the school has never left me alone and always given me the support I needed.

CHAPTER 6
MENTORING: BEING ALL THINGS TO ALL PEOPLE?

The following two chapters consider how schools offer support to NQTs by the provision of a mentor, that is a nominated individual who is given general responsibility for the oversight of the new teacher. They consider three main aspects of mentoring:

- the range of personnel who take on the mentoring role and criteria for their selection
- variation in mentoring activities undertaken with NQTs, including the timing and amount of time involved in mentor support
- the qualities mentors are expected to possess

In highlighting the key issues emerging from the data on each of these three themes, the research shows some significant differences between primary and secondary school mentoring. It is important to stress that the focus is exclusively upon the one-to-one relationship between an NQT and a particular designated staff member which, as Chapter 2 has shown, is likely to be only one component within the school's total induction system or 'programme'. Though the 'official' mentor is more often seen as the central figure in the support system offered to an NQT, a number of induction strategies - and other personnel - may also be guiding the NQT through his or her first year. It should also be noted that the term 'mentor' was not universally used - other labels, such as 'mentor-teacher', 'teacher tutor' or 'professional tutor' - were evident. In some cases, staff with these latter titles had official responsibility for coordinating several components of the induction process as well as personal supervision of an NQT. In others, professional tutors or teacher tutors worked with other staff who acted in a mentoring capacity. Some LEAs and schools have restricted the use of the term mentor to apply to those individuals who had a role with Articled or Licensed teachers. It is the nominated role of providing individualised support which is under consideration in both this chapter and the next.

Personnel undertaking a mentoring role

A first consideration for any school appointing a newly-trained teacher is to determine who will undertake any official mentoring role. Clearly, this choice will, at some level, reflect school managers' views on the purpose and outcomes of mentoring, and who, within the existing staff, carries the appropriate credentials for their particular interpretation of the role. Hence, as well as personal attributes, status may be seen as an important criterion in the selection of a mentor. Variations are likely to signal important differences in how the role is conceived and subsequently enacted.

A comparison of personnel undertaking an official mentoring role in the 30 case-study schools shows the extent of this variation (see Table 6.1).

Table 6.1: Status of designated mentors

Secondary (N = 12)		Primary (N = 20*)	
Deputy head	2	Headteacher	1
Head of department	6	Deputy head	6
Subject head	1	Allowance 'C'	2
Deputy head of department	3	Allowance 'B'	6
		Allowance 'A'	3
		Standard scale	2

(in two primary schools, two mentor-NQT relations were investigated)

Thus, the secondary sample showed a very consistent pattern of mentor selection - with a straight and unambiguous line management underpinning the mentor/NQT relationship in nearly all the case study schools. In some of the cases where heads of department (HoD) or deputy heads (DH) were ascribed mentor status and duties, it was said to 'go with the job'. In contrast, Table 6.1 shows that the status of official mentors in the primary sample was far more varied, ranging across the whole spectrum of staff (from ex-probationer to headteacher): though, in three cases, deputy heads also had acquired the mentoring role as part of their job description. Perhaps the greater variation in the primary school sample begins to intimate different criteria being applied to mentor selection, as well as reflecting the less hierarchical or flatter management structures which often characterise primary school staff-relationships.

In explaining the reasons underpinning the best choice for mentor role, respondents cited a number of factors to be taken into consideration. Put together, eight main factors emerged in underpinning mentor choice, some of which might suggest the advantage of not selecting high status staff while others are those which perhaps only more senior members could fulfil. These are listed in Table 6.2 and brief comments offered on each.

Table 6.2: Criteria for selection of mentors

- recent experience of being an NQT/probationer
- nearness or proximity (teaching in nearby classroom)

   direct linkage/overlap with NQT teaching commitments
   – (e.g. teaching parallel or similar age-ranged classes), expertise/experience directly relevant to NQT (e.g. pupil assessment responsibility; past teacher of NQT's class)

- non connection with an assessment (or direct line-manager) role/function
- a source of accurate information about school/department procedures
- a valuable role model
- capacity to effect change in school on NQT's behalf
- ensured commitment to/investment in the role.

Recent experience of being an NQT/probationer was cited as a valuable aspect of mentor support by a number of interviewees. Indeed, one LEA's suggested guidelines on mentorship made this criterion an official recommendation. However, it should be noted that in this case, the LEA itself played a strong developmental and assessment role in induction at school level, with half-termly visits involving extended observation, feedback and negotiation of an NQT 'focus' for development. Equally, the two primary schools who deployed their most recently qualified staff as official mentors also operated with strong year 'team' structures, and the headteacher in each case took a close interest in the progress of the NQT, with half-termly individual meetings to discuss development needs. Thus, these 'recency-factor' official mentors, offering strong pastoral support, operated largely in a 'buddy' type role. The overall structure of induction within which they worked was, in effect, a version of the tri-support system outlined in Chapter 2.

It should also be noted that the NQTs in the sample who advocated mentors' 'recency factor' invariably were those who had found themselves in mentoring relationships with high status staff in largely mono-support induction systems or those where the selection criterion of 'going with the job' was acknowledged. These NQTs' preferences for less high status staff often related to their unease at approaching busy senior staff with what might be deemed 'small and trivial problems' and how admission of difficulties would be perceived.

> *I think someone who has recently completed induction is more in touch with the issues and problems you face. Little things can get you down, they can build up and become major but some things are too trivial to bother the mentor, e.g. should I do up pupil's shoelaces.* (NQT: Primary.)

However, in other cases it was clearly stated that experienced official mentors were preferred:

Mentors need to have experience under their belt and a number of years at the school so they are familiar with school policy. (NQT: Primary.)

Its got to be somebody experienced so you can offer practical advice and support, mentors just out of college don't have the experience or advice to offer when there are problems. (Mentor: Primary.)

Nevertheless, the principle of some involvement of recently qualified teachers in induction and support was increasingly seen to have merit in a number of the case study schools, both primary and secondary. At the very least, experienced mentors noted that the 'psychological mobility' to empathise with the NQT's newness was an important aspect of their role.

Nearness or proximity was cited by a number of respondents as a particular advantage in the mentor/NQT relationship. Working in adjacent classrooms or adjoining teaching areas allowed NQTs to seek instant responses to issues and problems which arose in the course of their daily classroom teaching. Equally, it gave mentors an easier opportunity for supportive surveillance. In primary schools particularly, NQTs sometimes found they increasingly turned to a neighbouring teacher and an additional 'unofficial' mentoring role might develop, or even, virtually supplant the designated mentor. Indeed, in some cases, the lack of proximity was seen to prohibit the level of mentor support both asked for and received. Though proximity was mentioned less often as a component of effective mentoring support in secondary, it did feature among the recommendations of one induction coordinator, whilst one HoD/mentor referred to the value of having her work station sited next to her NQT's in the departmental office. Overall, consideration of the location of mentor and NQT might be seen as an important way to assist, if not entirely ensure, the quality and amount of support available. At the very least, school managers may wish to take account of the likelihood of an NQT utilising neighbouring staff as a source of support.

Direct linkage/overlap with NQT teaching commitments was often cited as a highly significant factor in successful mentor/NQT relationships. NQTs operating with their mentor in year teams (primary) or sharing modules (secondary) were consistently among the most satisfied with their induction year. The discourse which naturally accompanied joint planning and then implementation was greatly valued for developing practice - and reflection. One mentor not linked to her NQT's year team recognised this loss:

We work in different year groups, and in different parts of the school - and you get caught up in your own little world - I could have been of more

> *aid, [there's] a detachment from the NQT's specific teaching problems because of being in different years and teaching different levels [of the National Curriculum].* (Mentor: Primary.)

Where such natural partnerships were not possible, such as single intake primaries or very different timetables in secondary, mentors with expertise/experience directly relevant to the NQT also rated highly. Thus, one secondary NQT valued his mentor's pupil assessment responsibility (and indeed, when given the opportunity to select a mentor, used this criterion). In primary, the fact a mentor taught an adjacent year group or was a past teacher of the NQT's class was cited as being particularly useful.

Closely connected to this selection criterion could be added an overlap, or convergence, of **values** underpinning practice. Whilst this criterion of mentorship was rarely mentioned by any respondent, it was sometimes recognised as a factor in the success – or otherwise – of the mentoring relationship as a whole.

Non-connection with an assessment role was to emerge as a major issue in schools' selection criteria for the mentor role. At both primary and secondary level, a number of interviewees cited this as a key consideration:

> *Deputy level is not the level for mentoring - a deputy is not the person to whom an NQT can open their hearts, there's something judgmental about that tier, (it's linked to promotion too). No matter how neutral or supportive a DH was, NQTs might fear problems would be logged there.* (Deputy/mentor: Secondary.)

Overall, a noticeable trend across NQTs', middle and senior managers' accounts of the appropriate criteria for selection of mentors for the future was the move to involve less high status staff in mentoring or to reassess assumptions about more senior personnel/direct line managers undertaking the sole or main mentoring role. There was rarely an equivalent rethink to replace existing mentors with higher status staff. This 'devolvement' of the mentor role was invariably linked to the need to separate an assessment brief from the more supportive aspect of mentoring. It may suggest that senior staff were gearing up to a more detached assessment role, perhaps as LEAs' inspectors/advisers and the probationary year were no longer in place to perform the quality assurance aspect of induction. All in all, it appeared that a bi- or tri-support system was increasingly seen as the most effective solution to the perceived inherent contradictions in trying to fulfil both a non-judgmental support and assessment role, and that **'collective mentoring'** best met the various strands of effective individualised support and development.

A source of accurate information about school/department procedures may appear as a fairly self-evident criterion for mentor selection. As a secondary NQT remarked: *'A mentor should be someone who gives you a clear idea of what's going on in the school and department'*. From this, it might seem logical that teachers with considerable experience at the school were best placed to take on mentoring responsibilities. However, there were two examples (primary and secondary) in the case studies where teachers who were as new to the school as the NQT were deployed as mentors, by virtue of their status as deputy heads. In both cases, the plethora of new senior management responsibilities proved disadvantageous to the amount of time for support available to the NQT, particularly as the year progressed. Given the finding that the summer period was a crucial phase of induction, the efficacy of using new appointments in mentor roles might also be questioned. Notwithstanding this, an example of a **recent** appointee to a middle management role proved a highly successful mentoring relationship, as the mentor was able to encourage the NQT to work to procedures which she wished the department as a whole to adopt. Equally, some schools saw much advantage in holding joint induction sessions with NQTs and other newly-appointed staff, and one primary NQT pinpointed support another new teacher (subject coordinator) had given her, particularly about *'... worries of being new and settling into the school'*.

A valuable role model was cited as an important criterion for mentor selection in a number of cases:

> *I hope I've got some good practice that he can copy or learn from - I would like to think I could tell him what his priorities should be, or at least advise him on those .... I think perhaps the attributes of the mentor are more important than common subject matter - things like good classroom management are generic to all teachers.* (Mentor: Secondary.)

However, an alternative viewpoint on any role model responsibilities also emerged:

> *You need to set a professional example, such as be punctual, but you're not there as a role model - it's up to the NQT to build their own methods, ideals, ideas within teaching ... in teaching you've to develop your own approach at your own pace - as mentor, you're there to reflect the needs of the NQT, it's not **your** role that is important, it's what you can give, that's all - you're not there to show how good you are, you're just there to reflect and help wherever you're needed. You're not perfect.*
> (Mentor: Primary.)

This stark difference of opinion on the notion of a good role model being the major criterion for mentor selection opens up a key debate about the very purpose of induction support and mentoring. While some school managers emphasised that their induction programme, and the mentor's role within it, was a way of ensuring the NQT conformed to school approaches and values, others stressed that the induction process should support NQTs in determining their **own** professional development.

> *We look for an NQT who is amenable to ideas, open to our ideas and suggestions .. we'd want someone who would accept another teacher [the mentor] working with them for one or two hours a day and be prepared to take advice. We want people to work this school's way.*
> (Headteacher: Primary.)

> *I think a mentor is someone who is sensitive to the subtle issues which perhaps NQTs are not able to articulate well, or feels they can't say. The mentor needs to know the NQT as closely as possible. The relationship between mentor and NQT is one where, as far as possible, those needs and worries - the areas which an NQT finds it difficult to talk about - can come out.*
> (Headteacher: Primary.)

Clearly, there should be no inference that mentors selected for their capacity - and opportunities - to demonstrate exemplary professional practice cannot also perform the supportive role outlined by the second respondent. However, the different emphasis may suggest that schools need to think carefully how far they wish to directly influence and mould the NQT's practice and classroom performance, and whether 'good teaching' is the same as 'good mentoring'. Some respondents pinpointed where they felt the real skill of a mentor lay:

> *I will always get an honest and professional answer to my queries, my mentor gets me to reflect on choices and options. She'll say 'what do you think you should do? Why would you do that?' - it's true mentoring. She is a teacher and a nurturer. Yes, she encourages me to analyse, hypothesise and reflect - we're doing it every day even when we don't realise we're doing it.*
> (NQT: Primary.)

> *My mentor **listens** ... if I take a problem to other colleagues, they say 'I'd do this or this or this' - but I'm not asking them how **they'd** do it, I'm asking them to help me. It's actually listening to you rather than launching off into what they do. My mentor, in contrast, starts from my capabilities.*
> (NQT: Secondary.)

The capacity to effect change in school on the NQT's behalf was mentioned as a criterion of mentor selection mostly in those (secondary) schools which had applied the term 'mentor' to a senior manager with overall induction responsibilities. It invariably accompanied the admission of possible discrepancies and shortcomings in the quality of support which NQTs might experience from immediate colleagues or middle managers.

> *It's useful having a senior teacher as a mentor. The disadvantage is they are very busy, but the advantage is they have the clout, the authority and the power to get things done (and know the 'ins and outs' of school politics).* (NQT: Secondary.)

However, the sample did include a case of a main grade or standard scale primary mentor who acted as intermediary on behalf of an NQT in similar circumstances of conflict with an immediate colleague. This suggests that mentoring requires, if not status, at least some means to access senior staff as well as diplomacy or 'political' negotiating skills.

Ensured commitment to/investment in the role emerged as the final fairly self-evident criterion for mentor selection. Notwithstanding this, important points about the attitude of the mentor emerged in the interviews. The difficulty of finding **time** to undertake the role was the major issue, mentioned by virtually all respondents. Those mentors who expressed most commitment to their role, invariably recounted how it meant an investment of their own time, and how the willingness to do so was an important precondition of undertaking the role. Moreover, though it was frequently mentioned how the mentoring process was beneficial to mentors themselves in terms of development and reflection on one's own practice, this in turn required specific attitudes:

> *Mentoring is a very good tool to help your management role - listening skills, communication, (people) management. But, you have to give it your all - if you're not prepared to give it your own time, I don't think it will work. I think you need to **want** to do it, be open-minded enough to do it.* (Mentor: Primary.)

> *Don't do mentoring just because you've been asked, you can only support if you feel strong enough to give that support, there is a time commitment, and if you feel jealous of your own time then you can't do it. You've got to believe it's worthwhile, got to find it enjoyable and stimulating and you've got to feel sufficiently secure in yourself. You can't counsel someone if you can't meet your own needs, if you're feeling vulnerable yourself, for whatever reason, if you're feeling negative about your status, your job or anything then you should say no.*
> (Mentor: Secondary.)

The notion that mentoring requires a particular attitude set and above all personal investment in the role in some ways challenges assumptions that a particular level of management should or can automatically take on the mentorship mantle. Undoubtedly, within the sample, the strongest and most sustained mentor/NQT relations were evident in schools where there was a particular commitment to the role and where investment produced tangible personal and/or professional benefits. These included:

- **Professional development** e.g. a HoD who joined the school's staff development team in the light of his year of mentoring and expressed interest in moving into higher education and INSET work

- **Career advancement** e.g. a primary professional tutor who went on to achieve deputy headship or headship

- **'Psychic reward'** e.g. a primary deputy who described her personal sense of satisfaction and fulfilment in the professional growth of her NQT

- **Institutional strategic advantage** e.g. the new HoD who saw her NQT as a strategy for change within the department (the 'protégé principle')

This finding may suggest the need for senior managers to consider whom within their own staff might personally and professionally benefit from mentoring. Beyond that, successful mentoring may also depend on ways of ensuring such personally beneficial outcomes are strategically planned for (such as the possible promotion opportunities of mentoring being made explicit) or that the **time** committed mentors freely invest is replicated in more formalised ways.

The time to mentor

Having looked at the range of personnel undertaking a mentoring role, and presented a collation of views on appropriate mentor choice, this final section focuses on the amount of time given to mentoring and the timing of such support. Evidence is taken from the three termly interviews in which NQTs and mentors were asked to outline the kinds of mentor support offered and provide some details of the focus of discussions. Details of when and where such support occurred were also requested.

In the 12 secondary schools, five of the mentors arranged timetabled discussion time with the NQT in term one, though the amount and timing varied greatly.

Table 6.3: Time and timing of mentor support: secondary

	Mentor	Time and timing
School 1	HoD	Weekly meeting in mutual non-contact time (at least 1 hour)
School 2	DHoD	Weekly meeting in non-contact time (40 minutes)
School 3	DHoD	Fortnightly lunch time meetings (also a subject planning meeting) (35 minutes)
School 4	HoD	Daily in first few weeks + three weekly subject planning meeting (unspecified)
School 5	DH	Fortnightly lunch time meetings (about 20 minutes)

It was noticeable that by the second and third terms only one of these schools (school 1) had maintained the initial high level of formalised contact: in all other cases, some [negotiated] reduction in frequency or length of meeting was reported. However, fall-off was less evident when the mentor and NQT also utilised the agreed discussion time for specific subject planning. Here, there was clearly mutual benefit in the investment of time and a gradual development into 'equivalent colleagues' within the relationship was acknowledged.

In the seven other secondary schools, it was reported that there was no timetabled meetings: though one department head and her NQT stated they had deliberately opted for mentor-time not to be timetabled, preferring frequent extended discussion-time after school which 'arose naturally' or was at the request of the NQT. This mentor/NQT relationship continued an extended dialogue throughout the year.

Thus, in half of the twelve secondary schools the timing and amount of mentoring discourse was described with very little specificity. Typical comments included: *'we might have ten minute informal chats in the morning'*, or mentoring was by *'generally being available'* to the NQT; or it was suggested that general departmental meetings and social interchange was the main arena of mentoring. Significantly, in none of these informal, 'incidental' and ***ad hoc*** arrangements was there any reported ***increase*** in mentor discussion time over the year. In some cases, when asked to outline the term's mentoring process, some mentors and NQTs equated the formal observation of the NQT with mentoring.

In sum, the picture of mentoring in secondary schools was one of very different interpretations and degrees of time-investment in the role. Over the first term, and equally over the year as a whole, front-loaded support seemed a fairly typical pattern of mentor involvement. On one level, this is unsurprising - as NQTs successfully settle in and grow in confidence, the level of support is likely to decrease. However, it does perhaps indicate that the purpose of mentoring in many cases is seen as 'habilitating' the NQT rather than any continuous considered process of managing and extending their development. (This may in part give some explanation as to why profiles were not always easy to establish and maintain.)

The picture of primary schools' investment in mentoring time also shows variation in amount and emphasis. In the sample of 18 schools only four mentor/NQT relationships nominated specific timetabled discussion time throughout the first term (see Table 6.4).

Table 6.4: Time and timing of mentor support: primary

	Mentor	Time and timing
School 1	Deputy	A regular Friday, after school session for 1- $1\frac{1}{2}$ hours
School 2	Head of year	A 30 minute period of mutual non-contact time created if needed (support also included weekly observation)
School 3	Head	Weekly lunch-time meeting (altered to after school due to competing priorities)
School 4	Head of year	Weekly lunch-time meeting

In four other schools, weekly year group planning was identified as the main occasion for mentor support (as mentor and NQT both worked in or as a year team), and five referred to a single extended discussion to determine the use of NQT non-contact time for the term. In other cases, mentor discussion time was described as 'snatched', 'as and when', 'informal', occurring during lunch-times, 'occasional' assembly/hymn practice or after school. However, several mentors emphasised keeping daily contact with their NQT, especially in the first few weeks. Working in adjacent classrooms was likely to be a useful factor here. Letting the NQT be pro-active in seeking support and discussion time was also seen as a preferred way of mentoring in some of the schools and explained the lack of timetabled contact. Eight of the schools defined regular mentor presence in the NQT's classroom as a major component of their support process.

As with their secondary counterparts, mentors in primary schools usually reported a considerable reduction in time given to mentor discussion as the year progressed - again as NQTs grew in confidence and capability. The exception to this was where year group planning was equated with the mentoring process. Equally, timetabled classroom support tended to be continued, although sometimes it became a casualty of staff absence or other emerging commitments and competing priorities. These vicissitudes of a school year were also cited as a reason for the decreasing opportunity for mentor discussion time generally. Overall, the picture in the primary school sample corroborates the evidence emerging from the secondary school data: despite often enormous commitment from mentors themselves, there were very real problems in finding the time to sustain any discursive (or developmental) role with regard to an NQT's practice.

> *My main weakness as a mentor has been other demands, the lack of time has been a real problem. I feel I'm just paying lip-service to the role. I like to do everything well, and I hope I have but I feel I could've done it better if I'd had more time.* (Deputy HoD/mentor: Secondary.)

> *It would be nice for me to be offered the same non-contact time as my NQT so we could work and talk together. That doesn't happen and any sessions we have will have to be after school. That's difficult because we already have lots of meetings - we look in our diaries and often it's very difficult for us to meet. We find that because of our commitments we have to snatch time. So we never actually make up a development programme because we can't look that far forward.*
> (DH/mentor: Primary.)

> *There should be a regular slot to let mentors work alongside NQTs. It should be given priority and I feel I've let my NQT down - a regular meeting after school should also be given priority. With so little time, it's difficult to perform the mentor role adequately. I'd like release time to let me do my job properly ... it's fortunate the NQT is so good because otherwise the school would have to pick up the pieces.*
> (Allowance B/mentor: Primary.)

CHAPTER 7
MENTORS IN ACTION

The previous chapter established who was undertaking mentor roles, and that many of those doing so generally felt they had insufficient time to fulfil their role. This chapter focuses in more detail on the kinds of mentoring activity actually undertaken and discusses the perceived attributes and qualities which mentors should possess. It concludes by documenting four cameos of mentors in action.

Mentor activity

Looking across all 30 schools, six main **types** or **modes** of mentor activity were evident, and these are listed in Table 7.1. Only some of these types of mentor activity featured in both the secondary and primary schools. It was also evident that the emphasis of these different mentor modes of working varied: some mentor activity seemed primarily intended to **ameliorate** or ease the NQT's working conditions (including their 'frame of mind'); some to **analyse** and **develop** their practice; and some to directly **assess** progress. Mentors usually operated in more than one of these six ways or different individuals might perform several functions.

Table 7.1: Types of mentor activity

- Mentor as classroom support
- Mentor as classroom analyst
- Mentor as collaborative planner
- Mentor as induction programme negotiator
- Mentor as informationist
- Mentor as welfare monitor

Mode One: the mentor as classroom support

This mentor activity was found exclusively in the primary school sample, and involved the mentor operating as an additional teacher in the NQT's classroom. It was an explicitly participant role. Many references to being an 'extra pair of hands' or 'helping out' clarified that its main purpose was seen as a way of easing the NQT's teaching load and providing opportunities for the pupils of the NQT to receive additional attention and support in their learning. In this way, it was perhaps almost the primary school equivalent of decreased work load exemplified by extra non-contact or no form tutor responsibilities in secondary schools. However, it also allowed the mentor to undertake supportive surveillance or monitoring of the NQT, and to guide the NQT in issues such as match and differentiation. Sometimes it afforded the opportunity for the mentor to demonstrate their own classroom expertise as a role model. Hence, despite a rhetoric which often portrayed mentor classroom support as predominantly an **amelioration** strategy, it could provide important opportunities for **analysis** and **development** of practice (though, of course, as has been shown, opportunities for subsequent mentor/NQT discourse on this were very much rarer). More ambiguous would be utilising classroom support mode in any **assessment** capacity.

Mode Two: the mentor as classroom analyst

This mentor activity was essentially non-participant and involved the mentor observing and commenting on the NQT's practice. Observation procedures may be laid down in school or LEA guidelines or in a profile. Such analysis of an NQT's classroom performance was usually, but not exclusively, linked to assessment. In almost one-half of the primary school sample (eight schools), mentors had **no** involvement in observation whatsoever, and only three of the 20 primary school mentors described undertaking a classroom analysis role on a regular basis (i.e. other than as an agreed one-off formal assessment observation). In each case, some discomfort on the part of the NQT was registered. Indeed, in two instances, the classroom analyst mode was dropped and replaced by the less threatening classroom support role.

> *It's different [and better] this term, I think her role is now more one of support rather than criticism, though that's not the right word - whereas before it was more a matter of observing me and moulding me, the mentor's role is now much more one of support and working **with** me in the classroom.* (NQT: Primary.)

> *I feel more comfortable now it isn't a 'them and us' situation, my mentor is no longer coming in the classroom observing and making notes as she did in the first term. At the back of your mind you always think, well why? You put up some suspicious guard. I think I would tell her more things about how I feel now she's no longer observing me.* (NQT: Primary.)

All this suggests that the mentor as classroom analyst is potentially a high risk strategy, particularly problematic if undertaken too early in a developing NQT/mentor relationship. However, it was also evident that the classroom analysis mode was appreciated later in the year, although it may be this was predominantly for reassurance rather than development of practice.

> *My mentor was able to come in on one occasion this [second] term - she came and managed to observe a fairly typical session and the main outcome was reassurance that I was doing all right and that I was getting on well.* (NQT: Primary.)

In contrast to the primary school sample, in each of the 12 secondary schools, the designated mentor did undertake classroom observation, usually described as a once- or twice-termly event, and invariably seen as linked to on-going or **formal** assessment. The major problem reported by secondary school mentors was finding the time to do this classroom observation (particularly if a range of the NQT's lessons was to be seen), and the disruption to their own classes which it might involve. The observation/analysis had strong overtones of quality assurance, often seen to continue 'probationary year' procedures, rather than signal any major new departures into developmental or analytical activity. One exception was observation/classroom analysis linked to a competence-based profile in which significantly the school had strongly invested in training its middle management mentors. (Further comments on profiles are found in Chapter 9.)

Mode Three: the mentor as collaborative planner

As already indicated, a number of mentors - in both primary and secondary schools - saw a major and valuable aspect of their role as working in joint curriculum planning sessions. These mentors worked with their NQTs in year group teams in some primary schools, or shared modules and syllabuses in secondary schools. They could carefully nurture and guide the NQT through quite subtle aspects of the teaching-learning process in such a way as to rank as a highly developmental mentor activity.

> *Because we team teach, the NQT and I meet to plan weekly, we get together continually. We have a great deal of contact on issues like planning, assessment and moderation. It means her planning for progression of the children is quite sound. Working in a team definitely helps the mentor role.* (Mentor: Primary.)

> *We began by looking at what she was doing on a day-to-day basis - as well, we have a rota of meetings and every third week it's the NQT and I who have a history meeting. At first we used this time more generally as NQT sessions. Now I'm changing the focus to talk about curriculum planning. But I'm taking it slowly. For example, I haven't as yet asked her to write any materials, but at the start of next term we will evaluate what we've done with year x.* (Mentor: Secondary.)

Mode Four: the mentor as induction programme negotiator

This mode of mentoring was another which was almost exclusively found in the primary school sample. Certainly, it did not feature largely in any secondary school middle-management/mentor's repertoire - though senior managers i/c induction might take on such a role. It occurred mainly in those primary schools where NQTs had an entitlement of extra non-contact time. In extended individual discussion, the mentor (who might also have an official induction coordination brief) negotiated a programme of support and observation both within the school and in other schools; and monitored the NQT's usage of the release time. These diagnostic conversations thus helped NQTs to determine key inputs for their own development and the mentor usually undertook any necessary mediation, administration or organisation for setting up the programme.

> *We looked at the curriculum areas each of the NQT felt they would most benefit from some input. As a result of these discussions, I would see the curriculum co-ordinator concerned and arrange either for them to go in and observe or for the co-ordinator to work with the NQT in their class. School induction time could be used, or we may buy cover or when I had release I was able to use that to free the co-ordinators. So, I will have a discussion at the beginning of the term with each NQT to try and work out an individual programme. Sometimes they are not sure so I will make suggestions. I'm hoping to arrange a visit to other schools this term - ones which we have worked with before.* (Mentor: Primary.)

Sometimes the mentor role of mediator or 'broker', to guide the NQT to colleagues with relevant experience, occurred without these formal or official meetings.

Mode Five: the mentor as informationist

In this role, the mentor provided the NQT with significant details of school (or departmental) procedures, routines, and events (in the school calendar), e.g. parent's evenings, reporting. Most mentors' work involved some aspect of this information provision, although in some cases this responsibility was also met by a school's central induction programme or, in primary schools, from senior managers. The informationist role was likely to be very important and prominent in the early phase of an NQT's induction as school routines had to be internalised. Checklists of information for mentors to convey were welcomed in one LEA's induction support handbook, and several schools (and secondary departments) advocated devising their own comprehensive audit to ensure no areas of significance to NQTs were inadvertently omitted. This kind of information omission was sometimes acknowledged to happen, particularly in later phases of the induction year when, as the teaching performance of the NQT was deemed highly satisfactory, mentors might have had less regular contact with their NQT.

> *The NQT had gained so much in confidence, we'd already assessed she was a very competent teacher .. and with SATs and the NQT's after school clubs, it meant [in this second term] the mentor discussion time was slipping. We found that without that regular input, the NQT was making some very rudimentary mistakes - not in her teaching - but in the protocols within the school. It made us realise we weren't doing our job properly - we had to get that discussion time back on line ... you forget she is an NQT.* (Headteacher: Primary.)

> *I recognise the school had missed out on dealing with equal opportunities with our NQT. It's the policies that are on-going and not uppermost which may get missed, especially these hidden curriculum issues.* (DH i/c induction: Primary.)

> *There's been almost nothing for the NQT this term, I've been caught up in other things and unless the NQT comes to me, there's no contact beyond corridor greetings and occasional dropping into his classroom. One problem has been the NQT has had to rewrite over 60 of his reports. So, next year, I'll have formal meetings and will work through the school calendar - I've learnt my lesson from not doing these things - it comes back on you.* (DH/mentor: Secondary.)

Another aspect of the mentor as informationist emerged in discussions with NQTs and mentors: it was apparent that, in some cases, mentors did not significantly develop their role beyond this function - and even, on occasion, did not fulfil it entirely satisfactorily:

> *I get good support from my colleagues in the department. The organisation isn't quite right and there could be better communication between experienced staff who know what's going on and us, the NQTs who don't! Sometimes you don't know what's going on and it doesn't make you feel as though you are in control.* (NQT: Secondary.)

Mode Six: the mentor as welfare monitor

In this mode, the mentor responded to the on-going concerns of the NQT, at classroom level and also, importantly, took account of their physical and mental well-being. As with the informationist role, mentor as welfare monitor would, in effect, describe an aspect of mentoring undertaken by almost all the school sample, yet it also defines the sum of support in certain mentor/NQT relationships.

In some of these cases, it was noted by NQTs that they would like their mentor to take a more critical interest in their teaching.

> *I really want my mentor's opinion more, for her to point out anything not being done right. But I do appreciate the sense that I think of her as a friend.* (NQT: Primary.)

> *I feel I would like my mentor to tell me where things could be better in my classroom, but she said she didn't want to do that, though I'm sure she could deal with it sensitively.* (NQT: Primary.)

However, the importance of monitoring and ensuring the well-being of an NQT was universally acknowledged, as most respondents recognised that, for some NQTs, the strain and stress of beginning a full-time teaching career was a major issue. The mentor as welfare monitor thus emerged as an important aspect of the role, and any under-estimation or omission was sometimes recognised as a possible significant factor in the 'failure' of an NQT. Self-evident though it may seem, some schools strongly articulated how attention to the NQT's psychological and physical well-being was necessary to ensure the full potential of a valuable trained professional. Thus, the 'lowest' level of mentor support *'... mentoring is essentially about being a friend'* may become the lynch-pin or *sine qua non* of a developmental role.

> *We've realised that the crunch period for support is at the end of the first term or early second term and that there's a real danger in thinking an NQT is coping when inside they are saying they're not, but just going along with the consensus. We now stress this in our summer induction. We realise problems can occur for NQTs if they have their private or home life in a period of instability, then coping with the stress of the first teaching post is even more difficult. In the summer induction, we've encouraged the new NQTs to actively seek help and support ... the mentor [now separated from assessment] is increasingly going to be the central pillar of that support.* (DH i/c induction: Secondary.)

> *I have a constant concern for my NQTs - above all other demands, I always ensure I speak to them in the staff room; check if they are OK if they've been ill. I make a conscious effort to approach one sitting alone ... you grieve for losing an NQT from the profession, and I feel I'm a shelter for them to run to - against their own HoD and conditions if need be. As their DH [and mentor] [I'm] on their side, I have clout, you've got to have somebody who will fight for them and stand ground.*
> (DH i/c induction: Secondary.)

However, the **welfare monitor** role was not just evident where an NQT was experiencing problems of adjustment to full-time teaching: several respondents stressed that the mentor also had a particular role in supporting NQTs who were operating successfully:

> *The mentor has the opportunity to look closely at what this new person has to offer, and to say it **for** them - to, if you like, brag and boast for them. An NQT is not confident enough to say 'I'm good at that' - so, through the mentor, she's got school-wide recognition of her talents ... it's about bolstering that person's confidence, you want them to believe in themselves - they're never going to achieve and contribute to the school otherwise.* (Headteacher: Primary.)

The overwhelming majority of this sample of NQTs were said by their senior managers and mentors to show considerable ability and talent. As a consequence, the mentors operating as **welfare monitor** usually recounted reduction in contact with their NQT as the year progressed. Nevertheless, a very small number described keeping pace with the changing concerns of their NQT, offering support, advice and counsel throughout **a cycle of NQT concerns** which typically began with routines of the school and classroom management issues in the first term, moved to children's learning issues such as match and differentiation in the second term, and through to wider-school responsibilities, career paths, etc. in term three. In this way, **welfare monitors** who were consistent in operating responsively throughout the year could be providing considerable assistance in an NQT's professional progress and development.

Collective mentoring

In looking across the six main different modes of mentor activity, and how they each may contribute to the **amelioration, development** and **assessment** of the new teacher, it became apparent that certain tensions could emerge when one individual attempted to undertake mentoring activities which included **all** these aspects of induction. Most obviously, the role of welfare monitor may be difficult to reconcile with that of classroom analyst/assessor: whatever the rhetoric and ideal, the 'critical friend' might be a particularly elusive aim:

> *You need a second mentor who isn't your boss, someone in school who just takes an interest in you as a new person ... someone not interested in your performance in the classroom but just how you were getting on - you need someone who listens to what you're saying, who cares that you're feeling like that as a person and not just as team member, someone away and removed from the problems.* (NQT: Secondary.)

This tension seemed particularly the case when a number of mentors identified that their major problem with the role was the difficulty and delicacy of effecting change to the NQT's practice if things were not going well:

I'm not always able to see a way forward when an NQT thinks all is OK but it isn't - in trying to be a colleague and responsive to needs rather than an overseer, but if the NQT doesn't perceive they have needs then I'm not that good at saying this is what I think your needs are.

(Mentor: Primary.)

I feel I should be more supportive rather than him finding out by mistakes. But I still want to keep a good relationship with him, there is ground he needs guidance on but I would like my HoD to reinforce the areas he's having difficulties with - I still want to be in an advisory role rather than telling him it's time xxx was sorted out. (Mentor: Secondary)

Hence, when NQTs, mentors and senior managers were asked about the role, often their descriptions of mentor support moved on to include the contribution of other staff, and it was clear that though **schools** fulfilled **amelioration, development** and **assessment** of the new teacher, it rarely was expected that a single person would provide the full range of mentor roles or modes of mentor activity. The notion of 'collective mentoring' with colleagues corporately providing a full range of support, often emerged as a more accurate definition of how primary schools and secondary departments conceived and executed their induction responsibilities.

Mentor qualities

In this section, findings on the perceived attributes of 'good' mentors and mentoring are briefly presented.

During the three rounds of interviews, NQTs and mentors were also asked about the mentor qualities which they felt were most valued: in the case of mentors, an additional question was asked on what were seen as their own particular strengths (and weaknesses) in the role.

As an overview, the most consistently mentioned attribute (by both the primary and secondary samples of NQTs and mentors) was that of **listening**.

it's a preparedness to listen

ability to listen objectively

good listeners so they don't misinterpret what we're saying

actually listening, not launching off into what they would do

being ready to listen to exactly what she wants rather than what I think she wants

listening - it's devoting time to listen

Apart from the capacity to listen, other attributes were mentioned more by one sector than another. Table 7.2 give the 'Top Twelve Rankings' of mentor qualities from both the primary and secondary NQT samples. The listing ranks in frequency of response, and includes all attributes which more than one NQT mentioned, though it should be stressed that sometimes a single primary or secondary respondent mentioned attributes not appearing in their sector's ranking (e.g. one secondary NQT mentioned empathy with newness). Equally, it should be recognised these are not 'hard' findings: they represent slight - yet perhaps significant - nuances in the responses of a small sample. Nevertheless, the fact that **giving time** was mentioned most by primary NQTs, (whereas secondary NQTs referred most frequently to **showing genuine interest**) may reflect the lack of flexibility in primary timetables, and the obviousness of personally invested time which primary school mentors had made. Also noticeable was the primary school sample's greater reference to **affective** qualities and to mentor's demonstrating some **equivalence** in the relationship, for example, **being a friend; empathy; approachability.**

Unlike their secondary school counterparts, primary NQTs did not mention **neutrality** which may reflect the more explicit line management of many secondary mentor-NQT relationships, as might the high ranking of **showing genuine interest.** Secondary NQTs clearly valued the mentor who operated as more than a line-manager. Also exclusive to secondary school mentoring were qualities such as **being well organised** and **communication skills**, which suggested secondary NQTs' appreciation of the management role of their mentor.

Table 7.2: Mentor qualities valued by NQTs

Secondary NQTs	Primary NQTs
A mentor quality which NQTs value is (someone who is) ...	
• supportive/shows genuine interest/ always asks how I'm doing	• prepared to give quality time/ willing to find time for you
• a good listener	• a good listener
• honest/open	• approachable
• well organised/efficient	• someone to respect/look up to/ good at job
• non-judgmental/neutral	• someone you can trust/ feel comfortable with
• gives ideas/shares resources	• empathises with newness/puts themselves in your place
• offers reassurance	• a friend
• available	• honest/open
• someone you can trust/ feel comfortable with	• non dogmatic/ doesn't impose their views
• communicates skilfully	• gives ideas and resources
• accessible	• accessible
• gives practical advice/guidance	• gives practical advice/guidance

In contrast to their NQTs, both primary and secondary mentors ranked qualities such as **approachability** and **giving practical advice** as well as their own **experience/skills.**

Table 7.3 lists the six most frequently mentioned qualities of mentors that were most valued by mentors themselves.

Table 7.3: Mentor qualities identified by mentors

Secondary NQTs	Primary NQTs
A mentor quality which NQTs value is: ● experience/skills/strategies ● readiness to listen ● approachability ● giving practical advice ● anticipating problems ● responsiveness/flexibility	● approachability ● readiness to listen ● supportiveness/... 'just being there' ● experience/skills/strategies ● giving practical advice ● someone to confide in/honour confidentiality

Again, it is possible to detect a greater tendency to highlight the **affective/ protective** in the primary school sample, with reference to 'just being there', 'someone to confide in', and perhaps slightly less emphasis being given to their own expertise and directiveness.

Mentors in action: four cameos

Cameo One

School: 5-11 primary   154 pupils + 26 FTE nursery   8 staff   1 NQT
Mentor: Deputy head

Criteria for selection:
The new headteacher wanted *'new zest in the school'*, and saw the appointment of an NQT as *'a way to help me change the school from the inside'*. The criteria for selecting the deputy was ensured commitment/investment - *'she's the most willing to give time and effort in and out of school'* and as a role model: *'... the deputy and I share a philosophy and want the same things for the school, the NQT will pick up what our philosophy is and know what we strive for'*.

Time and timing of support:
During the first term, the mentor and NQT met weekly for at least an hour after school on Friday, with some reduction in this amount of 'formal' contact as the year proceeded. By the end of term 2, meetings had shifted to lunch-times and in other 'generally snatched times'. A diary of the first term's meetings was kept and selective use of the LEA profile was made. As well as that, the mentor described keeping daily contact with her NQT, especially in the first weeks, and ensuring curriculum co-ordinators approached and offered the NQT support.

Mentor activity:
No **classroom support** or **shared planning** role was possible, with the mentor having a full-time teaching commitment elsewhere in the school, and there was no opportunity made for the mentor to work in a **classroom analyst** mode. The role was one of being an **informationist** and **welfare monitor**: and yet, with the time invested in this essentially discursive relationship (*'... we just chat, go through our plan, discuss the week and any major problems or areas she need help with'*), the mentor was able to provide support, advice and encouragement to match and extend the growing confidence and capabilities of her talented NQT. Thus, having initially worked through issues like routines of the school, discipline and classroom management, the mentor also carefully nurtured the NQT's drama expertise. The offering of guidance on running an after-school club (in term one) culminated in term 3 with support and encouragement for the NQT's whole-school production. Hence, a very obvious **developmental** purpose, to help her NQT realise potential, was evident within these modes of mentoring.

Cameo Two

School: 7-11 junior   500 pupils   20 staff   1 NQT
Mentor I: Deputy Head   Mentor II: Year Group Leader

Criteria for selection:
The headteacher explained that the non class-based DH worked in all classes, and would provide classroom support to all new staff, as well as the NQT, *'we want people to work the school's way'*. Hence, a strong **role model** selection criterion. The DH's role was underpinned by that of the second mentor (year group leader) who had *'a key role in the areas of planning, marking and curriculum'* and thus fulfils the criterion of **direct linkage to teaching commitments** of the NQT. The school provided a checklist of different staff's induction and mentoring responsibilities. Moreover, the DH stressed she found observing the development of an NQT and the bonding she achieved with them *'absolutely wonderful and particularly rewarding'* suggesting a high degree of personal **investment** in the role.

Time and timing of support:
In the first term, the DH worked daily in the classroom of the NQT. In addition, the NQT worked with the year group leader in weekly team planning meetings (which DH also attended) and also received individual support from this second mentor during Friday lunch hour. By term two, such intensive support had lessened - with less frequent classroom support and no longer individual meetings with the year group leader being reported. The DH also stated there was a lessening of her 'one-to-one conversations' with the NQT, which tended to become more in response to specific queries.

Mentor activity:
The DH/mentor's availability and commitment to provide a high level of **classroom support** for the NQT was evident, and she stressed it also gave her *'a very good picture of how the NQT is progressing, just by helping out in the classroom'*. Specific support on match and differentiation, as well as classroom management and organisation, followed from this close supervision. Hence, both **development** and **assessment** functions were evident. The **curriculum planner** mode was offered by the second mentor, though some involvement of the DH in this aspect of mentoring was also reported. The DH/mentor's **informationist** and **welfare monitor** role was apparent: she attended central induction meetings held by the head for the NQT and other new staff, and had further meetings with the NQT on issues itemised in the school's induction checklist (e.g. parents), suggesting the need to *'reinforce issues in the checklist, because an NQT can't possibly take in all the information in a few sessions'*. It was the headteacher who guided the career development of the NQT: conducting a professional development interview with her in term 3, encouraging involvement in a school working party on the NQT's specialism and designating subject responsibility to the NQT in the following year.

Cameo Three

School: 11-18 secondary   1,270 pupils   70 staff   4 NQTs
Mentor: Deputy head of department

Criteria for selection:
Choice of mentor was, according to the senior teacher i/c induction, *'negotiated between SMT and each department'*, and this DHoD had experience of mentoring ITT students and previous probationers in the department. Some **investment** in mentorship was therefore anticipated. As mentor, the DHoD stated he hoped to convey good practice to NQT (hence **role model** criterion), and both the NQT and mentor welcomed the fact there was lack of connection to line-manager/**assessment** in this choice. The fact the mentor and NQT worked in **geographical proximity** (adjacent laboratories) was mentioned as an advantage and feature of the mentoring process.

Time and timing of support:
Timetabled weekly meetings in a final period of the day ceased by the end of the first term: the meetings then became largely *ad hoc* and occurred only at the NQT's request. The mentor's accessibility meant the NQT *'sought answers to questions there and then'* during the mentor's teaching time and *'... used him for off the cuff things'*. The mentor was described as 'always popping in and out' of the NQT's teaching area. A formal observation (with feedback) of the NQT by the mentor occurred in the second term.

Mentor activity:
This mentor operated largely responsively, as, in effect, a **welfare monitor** and his NQT confirmed the good relationship the two had formed. The mentor acknowledged he had not been able to fulfil a **classroom analyst** role, despite the fact that offering on-going structured support to the NQT's classroom practice would have been of great value. Given the mentor also had ITT commitments, time was cited as a major problem; as was the difficulty of remaining supportive and operating in a critical capacity. Equally, the mentor felt there was *'... not enough department help, telling the NQT what is available ... we need to look at the department to see that there is a package there'*: hence, the **informationist** role was also seen to have been insufficiently attended to.

Cameo Four

School: 11-18 secondary   795 pupils   62 staff   3 NQTs
Mentor: Head of Department

Criteria for selection:
The school was said to expect that *'a lot of the responsibility for induction is middle managers, both academic and pastoral'*, hence HoD automatically undertook mentoring role. The DH i/c induction commented that HoDs were expected to do observation (assessment) of the NQT, within their existing non-contact time *'... it's good staff development for them'*. The HoD was a recent appointment and saw the NQT as a useful ally in her attempt to effect change within the department. Hence, **investment** in the role was evident. Equally, the mentor had a **direct link** to NQTs teaching, with shared modules and parallel classes and **geographical proximity** in that their workstations were adjacent.

Time and timing of support:
Mentoring took place without any timetabled meeting: and it was a unanimous decision not to formalise the relationship in this way. The NQT felt she would 'resent' meeting officially, preferring *'... the opportunity to ask there and then'*, whilst the mentor stated a weekly session might exacerbate the *'... inevitable tensions as line manager - a sense of breathing down her neck'*. However, through the year, both stressed they had lengthy on-going discussions on issues ranging from classroom practice (e.g. mixed ability teaching and group work, marking, their shared modules), to timetabling and 'educational philosophy'. All this was operating within much general departmental discussion. Occasional more formal and confidential meetings (twice in term 2) were also reported. The mentor felt this unstructured mentoring arrangement worked because the two got on well personally, and also pointed out that they *'shared educational values'*.

Mentor activity:
As the mentor stated that she felt she was *'constantly asking the NQT if she was getting on and managing'*, this was an example of a very conscientious **welfare monitor** mode, although some shared **curriculum planning** also was evident. Equally, the mentor encouraged her NQT to observe within the department and discussions on visits to other schools occurred in term 2. Hence, the mentor as **individual programme organiser** was in part evident. The HoD regretted the lack of opportunity for a full **classroom analyst** role, commenting *'... a lot of what I say about her teaching is more a gut reaction/ feeling rather than based on systematic observation'*. One formal observation in term 1 and term 2 was reported. The **informationist** mode was also one where the mentor felt improvements could be made - citing the need for a departmental handbook and how details of procedures for resourcing lessons should have been made clearer. The HoD also commented on the lack of linkage to the school's induction programme and the lack of information about her mentoring role generally.

CHAPTER 8
SUPPORT FROM LEAs: INDUCTION PROGRAMMES

There are a number of ways in which LEAs support schools and NQTs during the induction phase of a teacher's development. This chapter and the next uses data from the case study schools and local authorities to focus on three major areas of LEA support:

- central induction programmes

- visits to schools by LEA personnel

- other means of supporting school-initiated induction (e.g. through the training of mentors and/or the production of support materials and profiles)

LEA induction programmes

The interim report of the project provided important national data on LEA induction programmes and these are reproduced in the Summary (see Appendix 1). It was found, for example, that all LEAs arranged an induction programme for NQTs but that there was considerable variation in the number of days each new teacher was entitled (and funded) to follow such a programme. There was a similar wide degree of variation in the six case study LEAs involved in phase two of the NFER project (see Table 8.1). LEA induction programmes have been recently criticised by HMI and although good practice **was** identified, concerns were also expressed. These concerns were particularly in relation to the effective use of time, the duplication of areas previously covered during initial training, the overly general and idealistic nature of advice offered, the lack of relevance to NQTs' immediate needs and the unnecessary overlap with school-initiated induction (GB. DES, HMI, 1992; GB. OFSTED, 1993). The most highly valued part of LEA induction programmes, which the NFER interim report also strongly emphasised, was said to be the opportunity for NQTs to meet with others and to share ideas and problems. It is the intention of this section to draw upon the case study data, especially from the interviews with the NQTs themselves, to gain a better understanding of the precise benefits new teachers derived from participating in an induction programme provided by the LEA.

Table 8.1: LEA induction programmes: average no. of days per term

	Primary	Secondary
LEA 1	5 days	$2\frac{1}{2}$ days
LEA 2	1 day	Residential weekend (Term 1 only) plus 1 day
LEA 3	1 day	1 day
LEA 4	Residential weekend (Term 1 only) plus 2 days	$\frac{1}{2}$ day
LEA 5	5 days	5 days
LEA 6	1 day (2 terms only)	1 day (2 terms only)

Benefits gained?

As with any form of off-site in-service training event or activity, the amount of benefit gained by an individual teacher depended upon such factors as the quality of the provision, its relevance to perceived needs and the degree to which other more pressing concerns were given priority at the time. The responses from the NQTs invariably made reference to one or more of the above factors.

New teachers in two of the six case study LEAs were provided with an induction 'entitlement' of one-half day non-contact time each week, which was to be used for both school-based and LEA-provided induction. The teachers in these authorities were therefore offered a substantial LEA programme **throughout** their first year. Teachers in the other case study LEAs were not provided with such an extensive, centrally-based programme. The key question, therefore, was the time spent on these central induction programmes worthwhile or whether it would have been more productively used in the school or the classroom. In broad terms, the NQTs reported the LEA sessions to be valuable, although their degree of usefulness varied depending upon the individual's previous experience and training. An infant school teacher, who was attending two half-day sessions every three weeks, remarked: *'their usefulness has varied. It comes down to how badly I need to know that information. Also different advisers/tutors have different ways of getting information across and some are more effective than others.'*

At the time of the second interview the same teacher, when asked to comment on the usefulness of the central programme, remarked that about 80 per cent of it had been valuable: *'it has been very useful and it has provided that link between what we learnt at college and practice in the classroom. The training hasn't just stopped on the completion of college and it's helped break us in, so that next year I'll feel confident to continue'.*

The issue of **relevance** to the classroom and **practical applicability** came up time and time again. Favourable comparisons were often made with initial teacher training experiences - the latter was seen as not being sufficiently practical, whereas the best LEA induction programmes were practitioner-dominated and full of useful advice and ideas that could actually be used in classrooms. New teachers were able to point to specific sessions they had attended which had impacted upon their own teaching practice. When asked what impact, if any, the LEA induction programme was having on his practice a teacher remarked:

> *Quite a lot I think. We are being exposed to many practical ideas and are able to use some of these in the classroom, e.g. where do the children start, what do they know, all these sorts of questions are being addressed. The LEA programme isn't only about reviewing what you've learned on your training course but also trying to put that into practice. Are the children learning? Are they making progress, etc?* (NQT: Primary.)

This infant school teacher also noted how the LEA had been very helpful by providing information on the location and availability of various resources (e.g. technology and maths centres). Advice had also been sought from an advisory teacher in relation to this new teacher's responsibility to develop schemes of work in physical education.

A teacher in another school in the same LEA remarked that some induction sessions had been better than others and had covered areas previously covered during initial training. Reference was made to a recent session on equal opportunities:

> *It was very good but I'd done virtually all of it during my B.Ed. It was a relevant course but I'd covered it. (We were only given the title of the session with no details of content.) The most useful sessions are those that provide lists of resources and give us ideas for activities that we can use in schools. These sessions are normally subject specific and some of the ideas (e.g. about listening to readers) I've been able to put into practice.* (NQT: Primary.)

Other teachers were less able to be so specific about the programme's impact:

I think the (LEA's) programme is very much like a curate's egg. A lot of it is well meaning and useful, but you never really know how useful it's going to be until you try to put it into practice. I think a lot of what you pick up on these programmes is what you might call material/ideas/ information, etc which you log 'in the back of your memory'. It's about practising new angles, new approaches and new ideas, and you do use these although it's difficult to know whether it's conscious or unconscious.
(NQT: Secondary.)

I think all of it rubs off whether it's induction or general school INSET. It does have an effect on your thinking and your practice. But it's a combination of little things. You could never say: 'my goodness this has altered the course of the way that I look at teaching!' So I suppose it's a gradual process of being exposed to different ideas, approaches, etc.
(NQT: Secondary.)

The impact of LEA induction sessions on practice was however not always positive. Where criticisms were voiced they centred predominantly around the notion of, **'Can I use this in the classroom tomorrow?'** Two examples - one secondary and one primary - illustrate what NQTs wanted to gain from induction sessions:

Example 1:

A secondary teacher spoke disapprovingly of an afternoon she had spent with other NQTs and the subject adviser. The session had proved unproductive because the NQTs had been 'lectured to' instead of being allowed to discuss their own ideas. The teachers felt they were being presented with *'ideals we've all heard a million times before... and we don't need to talk about those, we need to talk about how things really are, we know the theory. it's putting it into practice we need help with'*. Although six NQTs attended the session *'it felt like we were only allowed to speak for about five minutes'*. Also the NQT wanted to raise discipline as an issue *'but the agenda of the meeting seemed pre-set by the advisory staff'*.

Example 2:

Two NQTs from the same middle school had attended an induction day on information technology and had returned 'very enthusiastic after that session'. The school's induction manager also remarked, that they had attended a twilight session arranged by the LEA on assessment and recording. The evening unfortunately clashed with a parents' evening at the school but the induction manager persuaded both to attend because of the high regard she held for the inspector. She remarked:

> *Unfortunately after only a ten minute introduction he handed the session over to a primary school teacher. Her session was apparently quite de-motivating in the sense that she had done everything and (the NQTs) felt that they could never, ever be quite as good as this teacher. Instead of perhaps easing them into things and giving them a simple view of how to approach this they got the opposite. It was as if they had to immediately take on board this enormous task and they came out of that session feeling completely deflated. This was most unfortunate as we persuaded them that the session would be well worth attending!*

The NQT involved in the research made a similar point and reiterated the need to ensure that what was offered by the LEA - be it during the day or after school - had to be seen as of immediate practical benefit.

> *I went to an evening session on assessment. This was a bit off-putting as they put this super teacher out front who told us about everything she was doing. I think it would have been more beneficial if we had had the opportunity to talk to other NQTs to see how they were doing. There is no way I could do all of that with my class. For example to spend ten or 15 minutes with any one child. Obviously this particular teacher was doing this and full credit to her but it simply would not have worked in my situation. It would have been better to have considered ways in which we could practically do such things in our classrooms. The LEA days have concentrated very much on the ideal and what should happen as opposed to the realities. It would be better if we had people putting forward suggestions as to various things we might like to try. The other NQT (at this school) attended this session with me and had very similar views.*

It should be said, however, that in general, NQTs highly valued the use of experienced teachers in LEA programmes. Such teachers were increasingly being involved in developing LEA induction programmes. For example, in one of the LEAs with a substantial centrally-based programme, the authority's induction coordinator had set up working parties to devise separate programmes for primary and secondary phases. The working parties were composed of senior school staff along with an ex-probationer or two. In one of the case study schools the deputy head, who was a member of the primary group, explained how the programme had originated, partly as a result of the negative feedback that had previously been received.

> *The probationers (as they were then) were unhappy with certain aspects of the (LEA) programme. They felt much of what was offered was simply regurgitating what they'd had at college over 4 years. Each week I made a point of seeing them to discuss matters, go through their files and deal with planning. I found that there were major areas that hadn't been covered during their training - so although they may have covered some*

*areas (e.g. reading) it had all been very theoretical. They wanted much more practical advice ..... We discussed (this concern) with the LEA and asked if next year's programme could focus much more on **the needs of the NQT** and to get the balance right between the in-school programme and that of the LEA ....To sum up, probationers were telling us, if I can use a cliché, that they were looking for 'tips for teachers' or very practical advice. When faced with 32 children how do you do this, etc? ... We felt deputies and professional tutors needed to be involved in developing (and running) the programme as experienced practitioners who could concentrate on the practical side of things. We also looked at the areas probationers had identified as crucial and we wanted to make sure that what we were offering came in the right sequence (e.g. classroom organisation and management in the first term). NQTs' responses to the sessions we've run so far have been very positive - practical and ideas to take away and work with. It has been hitting the right spot at the moment.* (Professional tutor: Primary.)

During a later interview the same professional tutor remarked that every effort had been made to meet the needs of NQTs. Before commencing employment in the authority each NQT had been asked to complete a profile of their training experiences so that the induction programme (both within the school and the LEA) could respond to any identified gaps. These profiles were collected during the LEA induction day in the summer, analysed and used to inform the programme from September. Much effort had gone into identifying NQTs' needs by asking the new teachers themselves what they wanted from an induction programme:

NQTs are in the best position to understand what they want at the end of the induction year, than say in October or November. We are therefore in a position to say that this is a programme that we've chosen based on last year's NQT experiences - recognising that 'wants' don't necessarily reflect 'needs'. .... The end result (we hope) will be the delivery of a quality programme but it's essentially down to the schools whether or not they buy into that programme. We have to be sure that what we produce is what the consumer wants. (Professional tutor: Primary.)

The need for differentiation

Given the wide range of age, experiences and backgrounds of NQTs it was said to be increasingly difficult to provide a programme from which **all** would derive benefit. A so-called 'blanket approach' was recognised to be no longer tenable. Notwithstanding some degree of choice or options within a programme and more details available concerning the content of the sessions, it was difficult, if not impossible, to meet the needs of everybody. As a secondary NQT remarked: *'if you had 200 NQTs you'd need 200 different programmes!'* A headteacher in another LEA made reference to the need for the LEA to adopt *'good primary practice'*:

> *I do feel that LEAs should be able to target their support and induction much more to the needs of individuals than to groups of 80 or whatever. I'm not sure how. If you looked at that in terms of good primary practice if you're always giving 30 children the same diet across the whole 30 children, you can't possibly be meeting the needs of the more able and less able children at the same time. And I suppose it is the same with newly qualified teachers. They all have different needs...certainly those who've been on a B.Ed course will have different needs to those who've been on a PGCE course.* (Headteacher: Primary.)

The need for differentiation of training to reflect differing levels of experience and expertise was also noted by a mature entrant who remarked how, as teachers, they were expected to acknowledge and understand that any class - even a banded or setted class - had a range of ability based upon knowledge and experience yet such thinking was not being applied to them as NQTs. *'It's as if (the LEA is saying) this is what you should be doing...by the way we're not going to apply it to you'.* Some of the LEA induction programme had been useful but so much depended on *'when you were starting from'*:

> *I've found getting out of school and listening to others, absorbing information, etc has, to a certain extent, been nice - pleasant, relaxing. It's 'headrest' time. The other NQT in the department finds it a complete waste of time because it's not focused on individual needs. My background, age and experience is very different from someone who's gone straight from school to college to school. For example, I just do not need sessions on classroom management - there are plenty of other areas where I could do with some assistance but not that. For some people it was all very new and useful. I could be more altruistic about it and say I'm part of creating that environment in order to help fellow professionals develop. Fine, but I also need developing myself. The same criticism could also be pointed at the PGCE.* (NQT: Secondary.)

Nevertheless, as will be suggested at a later stage, it was not always the **content** of the LEA programme that was seen to be the crucial factor: the function of providing social and emotional support might be as important as providing opportunities for professional and curriculum development. Indeed, professional development is less likely to occur in a situation where the new teacher feels insecure, isolated, lonely and unsupported.

During the course of the interviews over the induction year, NQTs were asked to comment on their needs at that particular point in time. It was clear that the needs of NQTs and their **'stage of concern'** changed quite considerably from term to term. In broad terms, their needs initially focused on matters relating to their own survival in the classroom and whether or not they were doing what the school expected of them. It was more common during the second and third term in post for NQTs' needs to be more differentiated; as confidence was gained they felt more able to focus on particular areas and issues relating to the curriculum and teaching and learning.

> *I think a lot of last term was about coping with the class and the new job. My needs were therefore more on the emotional side (if that doesn't sound too pathetic). It was all so new that I think I needed more emotional than practical support from the school. I find that this term I'm more aware of what I'm doing and more confident so any need I now have would be more practical and about developing my curriculum expertise.* (NQT: Primary.)

> *I think my needs at the outset were essentially about surviving. My needs focused very much on surviving and any help that I could receive was appreciated. In the Spring term my needs have been more concerned with whether or not the strategies that I have employed are working and will they work with the new children, the reception children. Are the strategies that I've used for class organisation and for approaching the children any good, will they work again? So it's more a question of this and seeing how the children have responded to different techniques.* (NQT: Primary.)

For some NQTs, no matter what was provided - be it by the LEA or the school - it was crucially important that certain key areas were covered:

> *Essentially I think whatever we do, there are 3 main areas which are a concern for all NQTs. In fact, I think they are concerns not only for new teachers. The '3 headaches', as it were, are: assessment; behaviour and discipline; and differentiation. I think all the rest you can more or less mug up on.* (NQT: Secondary.)

This same teacher went on to say:

> *I'm more concerned now with such things as differentiation, whereas before it was more a matter of survival and coping and disciplining the children. I'm not sure about this but do you just get used to things at a later stage which before you simply abhorred? To my mind experienced teachers are not really doing all that much better than I am, for example, in relation to discipline. So I guess I have concerned myself less with these sorts of matters and focused much more on other things which I suppose in general terms might be called 'quality of learning'.*

A teacher in a different school remarked: *'I think the kind of support I need now (from both the school and LEA) is more specialist, for example, concerning assessment or differentiation. The support I'm getting has changed to reflect this.'*

At this point it is worth noting the findings of the recent HMI **'New Teacher in School'** survey. The new teachers were asked at the end of the induction year to identify what they considered to have been their major needs during their **first** term of teaching. In order of importance these were:

- personal support and encouragement from more experienced colleagues
- help in learning about school routines and, in particular, pastoral systems and their own roles in pastoral teams
- support in lesson preparation and planning
- help with classroom control and discipline (GB. OFSTED, 1993.)

Such needs could, of course, by met by either an LEA or a school-based programme or, ideally, by a combination of the two working in partnership. Induction managers and coordinators in the NFER case study schools were asked to comment on the extent to which school- and LEA- induction programmes were coordinated and complemented each other. There was a general recognition that this was desirable but not always successfully achieved. Coordination was helped by the fact that details of the programme were made available to schools in the summer thus enabling the school's programme to complement and augment that of the LEA. However, there was said to be a need for more details than currently provided in order to achieve a better 'fit'. In some schools, NQTs met with their professional/teacher tutors and mentors in order to plan how to use their non-contact or induction time in school bearing in mind the programme being offered that term by the LEA. The time available for induction was limited and it was therefore seen as crucial to avoid any unnecessary overlap between programmes.

For some there was recognised to be a certain degree of overlap between school and LEA provision but that this was deemed necessary as both took slightly different perspectives. An induction manager who was a member of the LEA's team responsible for the secondary programme remarked:

*There is an attempt to coordinate the two programmes. Obviously if we're sending people out we know it months in advance. I was involved in drawing up the LEA programme and the school programme tries not to repeat what's in the LEA's programme. Any LEA programme has to talk about things in its widest context (e.g. special needs) but the staff here need to know about special needs provision in **this** school, how to* *identify youngsters, the system we use, the back-up here, etc. They should complement each other to some extent but the school programme is more determined by the programme of events i.e. the timetable of the school. For example, parents' evenings are coming up and I therefore have to make sure they've had something on this.*

(Professional tutor: Secondary.)

The question of timing - to reflect forthcoming important events, such as parents' evenings and report writing - was of obvious importance but it was not always the case, in either school-based or LEA-provided programmes, that such topics were considered at the most appropriate time.

Flexibility and responsiveness of the programme were also mentioned as important factors. Although school managers welcomed early details of forthcoming LEA sessions there was also a recognition that effective induction was negotiated rather than 'done to' or imposed on new teachers. Some LEAs not only offered a menu or choice of sessions and workshops but also were very responsive to the wishes of NQTs. The summer programme for secondary NQTs in one LEA, for example, was arranged only after NQTs and induction managers were consulted, whilst the summer primary programme revisited some of the areas and issues, earlier covered as a result of specific requests by NQTs.

The issues of applicability and relevance were also frequently raised. Most LEAs provided separate programmes for primary and secondary NQTs with the latter often having a combination of general and subject-specific sessions. Primary NQTs were not usually divided into age-specific groupings (e.g. early years, juniors) although frequently the sessions recognised that some matters were of greater concern and relevance to one category of NQT rather than the other. It was not uncommon, for example, for practical activities to be focused on either the early years or junior phases. Such differentiated provision was not always found, however, and although initially not welcomed by primary NQTs it was recognised that, for career purposes, it was unwise to restrict one's expertise to a particular age-range of pupils. It was also recognised that bringing together teachers of upper and lower primary classes was helpful as, with the National Curriculum, knowledge of the **whole** spectrum of learning was necessary.

As far as the secondary phase was concerned there did not appear to be a clear consensus in favour of the subject-specific rather than the general induction sessions. Different NQTs had gained from both to varying degrees depending upon their own training needs at the time. For example, an NQT was quite critical of a general session attended which was not perceived to have been sufficiently relevant to the secondary sector. He commented: *'It was like the old alligator and swamp story - if an alligator is snapping at your heels you tend to forget that you're here to drain the swamp! So the more secondary orientated sessions I've found to be the more valuable.'* In another LEA, the subject advisers were responsible for putting on training courses for their NQTs. In the past general sessions had been offered but were so poorly attended they had been disbanded. New teachers were said to be *'not really interested in the macro-level of LEA policy but more in the micro-level of their own school'*. Anything that did not relate specifically to the NQT's classroom situation was not highly valued. Similarly, secondary NQTs held differing views about the usefulness of **cross-phase** as opposed to **phase-specific** sessions. Again relevance and applicability were of overriding importance.

Certainly, it was the **quality** of the provision - covering such general areas as classroom management and organisation, discipline and behaviour, parents, and pupil assessment - that was a key criterion, along with the programme's overall relevance to practice in school. Sessions that were able to build upon NQTs' experiences in schools and provide opportunities to work with others from the same subject areas or similar age-ranges were highly valued.

Minimising disruption and workload

At the end of the day NQTs voted with their feet. If what was offered by the LEA programme was not deemed to be worthwhile or valuable then attendance would be affected. It was recognised, however, that the factors of quality, relevance, applicability and practicality were not the only ones that entered into the equation. Also of crucial importance was the issue of **what was not happening** as a result of NQT attendance at LEA induction sessions. In the same way that research into INSET and cover arrangements has found staff increasingly reluctant to attend training sessions during school time because of the work it generated both before going **and** on return to school (Brown & Earley, 1990), NQTs similarly commented on the extra work that could be created simply by attendance. Where possible NQTs absence from school to attend induction sessions was planned to minimise possible disruption to teaching - primary NQTs' classes would be covered, for example, or secondary NQTs timetabled to have little or no class teaching on induction days. This was not always achieved however and could create additional problems and increase the pressure on new teachers struggling 'to keep their heads above water'.

A secondary teacher made an interesting comparison between off-site induction sessions and whole-school professional development days:

With INSET days the whole school closes down; this is not the case when we go to the Teachers' Centre - the work doesn't stop or your classes cancelled simply because we are at the Teachers' Centre. It's like doing a long distance run and having to stop to get a stone out of your shoe. You've got all that to catch up again haven't you? Alternatively, you can plan it and run a bit faster to start with ie. get all your jobs done ahead of time and arrange for teachers to take your classes, then you can afford the time to stop and get the stone out. With an INSET day on the other hand, the whole school stops so you don't have this problem. Fortunately the LEA days are not always held on the same day of the week so it's not always the same pupils who suffer. (NQT: Secondary.)

The school did not close down in the NQT's absence; neither was their work load accordingly decreased. It was very often a matter of priorities and any ambivalence directed towards LEA programmes had to take account of the fact that the NQTs were working very hard and their prime concerns focused on the school, their class(es) and survival. As the induction manager from the same school as the above teacher remarked:

The NQTs themselves are sometimes ambivalent about the LEA courses but this is for the same reasons as I've mentioned before - a question of priorities and having lots of things to do - it's another meeting! When you're an NQT you are often very conscientious and become very aware of how much the pupils want you in their lessons. When you are out on courses there's a distancing that occurs between the teacher and the pupil. Continuous absence can have quite a bad effect on your relations with the class, so I think there's a lot of pressure on NQTs from pupils for them to stay in the class. (Professional tutor: Secondary.)

When attendance at LEA induction sessions was perceived to be adding to rather than alleviating the NQT's predicament and workload, alternatives were being considered. The most commonly considered were residential weekends and twilight sessions. The latter were rarely welcomed - often being seen as 'yet another meeting to attend' - but the former, found in two of the case study LEAs, were reported to have been very successful. In one case the residential had been organised by the LEA and in the other by several secondary schools for the NQTs in the area or division. Senior managers responsible for induction, were beginning to see the advantages of residential weekends in terms of helping to generate a sense of loyalty to the school and LEA on the part of the NQTs, relieve some of the pressure on their working week and eliminate any potential conflict between a commitment to the pupils and/or the LEA programme.

Newly-qualified primary teachers in a metropolitan borough were divided into two groups and asked to attend a residential weekend in their first term. This was organised by the primary adviser (since retired) and was generally well received. It had provided *'real contact with other NQTs'* which, according to one of the interviewees, would not have happened just as a result of a day at the Teachers' Centre. She remarked that:

> *Without the residential experience, contacts would be superficial and light and the NQTs wouldn't talk out their problems and classroom concerns openly and honestly as has happened. Also the weekend made you want to try new things - the challenge of rock-climbing (and other outdoor activities) generally has given us the confidence to try new things in the classroom.* (NQT: Primary.)

Interestingly, this same teacher had been requested to join a group (consisting of one-third of all primary NQTs) set up by the LEA to review the year's induction programme. For one half-day the NQTs were put in small groups and asked to discuss the pros and cons of different aspects of the year's provision. *'The general consensus was that the residential was definitely thought to be worth keeping on!'* Whether or not schools would be prepared to meet the costs of such in-service training is, of course, a significant factor.

Value for money?

The cost of subscribing to the LEA's induction programme (with or without a residential component) was becoming a major concern. As funds were gradually being devolved to schools, it was becoming apparent, especially to those (mainly secondary) schools with many NQTs, that the cost of the operation was becoming increasingly prohibitive. As several induction managers remarked, could they really afford to continue to subscribe to the programme offered by the LEA? Were there not other more cost-effective ways of providing comparable induction provision? (See Chapter 10 for a discussion of resource management. The issue of providing training outside of school time and payment for INSET is considered in Brown and Earley, 1990.) Partly in recognition of the concerns of the schools, twilight induction sessions were being introduced in at least two LEAs for next year's induction programmes. How successful they would be was, of course, unknown although both authorities were well aware of the patchy attendance of after-school sessions that had been arranged for mentors and induction managers.

Respondents were also aware, however, that, for some areas and issues, the LEA was often in the best position to provide training. Within LEAs there was a body of expertise – both in terms of subject or content **and** in working with teachers – to which schools had access. For example, primary headteachers remarked that NQTs often had little training in subject areas, such as PE, dance or art, and that it was not realistic or cost effective to expect schools (or consortia) to provide the necessary time and resources to meet these training needs. It was not that individual schools or consortia could not cover most of these needs, it was more a question of efficiency of resources and cost-effectiveness. As an induction manager remarked: *'the*

LEA can do things centrally more economically - it will become burdensome, time-consuming and "hitty-missy" if left to individual schools'. It was also said that schools often did not have the latest information or the requisite knowledge and expertise that was found in LEAs. An LEA programme was seen as bringing consistency and coherence to the areas being addressed, whilst also giving NQTs access to specific expertise (e.g. assessment, special needs, equal opportunities, National Curriculum) and providing a perspective that went beyond the school, thus combating insularity. It was also able to provide (in some cases, substantial) quality time to enable NQTs to deal with issues, to keep up to date, to be exposed to new ideas and good practice, and to provide opportunities for reflection. It was said that NQTs required time away from their schools to reflect on and evaluate their own development and practice - good LEA induction programmes enabled this to occur and offered an overview that schools could not so easily provide.

The importance of contacts

All those involved in the research agreed, albeit to varying degrees, that there was a need to provide an opportunity for NQTs to come together with fellow NQTs. Whilst some particularly valued 'quality time' for opportunities for in-depth reflection away from the classroom, for others it did not matter so much **when** or **how** such meetings took place provided that they **actually occurred**. This is an unsurprising finding bearing in mind what HMI and other research into induction has repeatedly highlighted. There were, nevertheless, several issues raised which have significant implications for those responsible for the organisation of such meetings, either within LEAs or schools.

The NQTs in the NFER study were asked to indicate how important it was for them to develop and maintain contacts with other NQTs, either in the school or the LEA. For many, particularly the single or sole NQT in a primary school, such contacts were crucial:

It's of life-saving importance! It's necessary to get together with other NQTs to recharge your batteries and to ensure that you don't feel a useless failure. (NQT: Primary.)

It's good to meet up with others but you have to be careful they don't end up as general moaning sessions. (NQT: Secondary.)

Going to these induction sessions makes you realise the grass isn't always greener! (NQT: Secondary.)

It's very important to have some time away from the front line and to meet up with others and realise they're under the same difficulties as yourself. It's also good to meet them socially. (NQT: Primary.)

The latter teacher when asked during the third school visit to describe why meeting with other NQTs was so important, commented that he did not socialise with other NQTs outside of the LEA induction sessions but remarked that over the induction year conversations with fellow NQTs had changed from *'Oh God!'* to *'Let's share ideas'*. This notion of the sharing of ideas and gaining support from each other was mentioned frequently and it was suggested that the 'content' of these central sessions was often of far less value than the contacts made and the opportunities created for sharing concerns, problems and ideas. Criticisms were levelled against sessions which did not take account of this or did not attempt to build such 'sharing' into any planned programme. One primary programme, for example, encouraged participants to bring something along to the session to share with others and had, very successfully, drawn upon the collective expertise of the group, whilst also providing significant and valued input.

Of course, the value of contacts with fellow NQTs which an LEA induction programme provides, depends significantly on the individual NQT's situation in his or her host school. Indeed, this was recognised by some of the case study participants. As a primary NQT remarked at the time of her first interview: *'I'm fortunate to be working in this school and I appreciate this when I talk to other NQTs on induction 'days'. Some say they are having problems and they rely far more on the LEA sessions than I do.'* For a number of reasons this teacher had been unable to attend most of the LEA sessions in the summer term. She was asked at the time of her third interview if she had missed this contact with other NQTs.

> *No, not really I haven't and I think this is because I've got on here so well with the staff. We have worked well together and supported each other during the SATs. There has been in-school support from the Head, the special needs person and the welfare assistants. We had a training day in the school on SATs plus the school sent me for a day at the Teachers' Centre so I haven't missed contact from other NQTs but I think these would have been much more important if I hadn't been working in such a supportive school.* (NQT: Primary.)

It is precisely those teachers who receive little or no support from their schools who will most miss LEA programmes should they disappear. In secondary schools, where frequently more than one NQT is appointed at any one time and for whom usually there is a formal induction programme (see Chapter 4) it is less likely to be a problem than for primary schools.

Senior staff were conscious of the support - professional, psychological and social - that regular external contact provided. However, even in those schools which supported NQTs, there was a need for them *'to let the mask drop'*. A primary head explained that all NQTs play at the role of being a confident teacher with children, parents and colleagues and they therefore need an opportunity to drop this persona:

> *I'm assessing the NQT so she can't drop the mask totally, so is the mentor in a way. It's difficult (for the NQT) to be 100 per cent honest - hence the opportunity to get away from school is good - the other NQTs (she meets) are people who won't necessarily know them all that well in the future. It's difficult for NQTs to complain about the head, the school or conditions in front of colleagues ... so I think it's a vent, a release, an opportunity to talk problems with someone who isn't a threat, or in authority or an employer ... everyone (at this school) is senior to her, I suppose.* (Headteacher: Primary.)

If the LEA was to no longer provide such a service for NQTs then it was suggested that the schools themselves would have to organise meetings for NQTs on a cluster or regional basis. In fact, this was already happening in those LEAs where extensive induction programmes were not found. For example, it was asked: *'How long would it be before one experienced teacher per school was released each term to "induct" the cluster's NQTs?'* As mentioned in the previous section however, there were said to be some things the LEA offered which schools would find very difficult to replace. In addition, providing opportunities for contact with other NQTs was seen as *'yet another responsibility that schools would be expected to take on'* and *'how many balls can you have in the air before you drop one?'* Total responsibility for the induction of NQTs was desired by a few induction managers but most were happy to see this continue to be part of the LEA's function. Senior staff wanted to be able to make use of those parts of the LEA programme that were most valued and, as such, welcomed the greater choice that the devolvement of induction and INSET funds would bring. They were equally aware, however, that such selective use by schools was likely to lead to the loss of expertise and the possible decimation of the whole LEA programme. (For a further discussion of teachers' views on the 'privatisation' of INSET, see Harland *et al*, 1993.)

In one of the case study LEAs, the funds for induction were to be devolved to schools so that for each NQT appointment the school was to receive £1500. These funds were in the form of vouchers and could be used for supply cover. Schools could, however, use the vouchers in ways that they chose - for example, to 'buy into' LEA induction sessions, to free induction managers or mentors or indeed, other ways which the school felt would best meet the needs of the individual new teacher. The fact that schools increasingly would be 'in the driving seat' regarding the purchase of induction and other forms of training was often noted. In the past LEAs had provided a minimum entitlement for **all** NQTs - they had at least ensured some equivalence of provision. Heads, therefore, were concerned that although they would *'give induction the priority it deserved'* they were not quite so sure this would be the case in all schools. In the words of a primary head:

If it's left to schools then variation in the amount of induction support will invariably result. The LEA (currently) provides a minimum entitlement for all NQTs .... there must already be an enormous variety in what schools offer. If we're talking about professional development, fairness, supporting people just coming into teaching (which is a very difficult period for them) then I think it's not acceptable for that provision to vary so much. LEAs must ensure some equal provision.
(Headteacher: Primary.)

For this reason, some LEAs were increasingly focusing on ways in which they could support school-initiated and school-managed induction, and it is the production of support materials, mentor training and profiles that is the concern of the following chapter.

CHAPTER 9
SUPPORT FROM LEAs: ASSESSMENT, MONITORING AND PROFILING

Whereas the previous chapter gave attention to the support provided by the LEA in terms of the provision of central induction programmes, this chapter concentrates on several other important aspects of LEA support. Its focus is on how LEAs have worked with schools to support school-initiated induction with particular reference to visits made by LEA personnel to observe teaching practice and to monitor school support. The chapter also gives consideration to the other main forms by which LEAs support school-initiated induction, such as the training of mentors and the production of support materials and profiles.

Visits by LEA personnel

An important aspect of LEA support in relation to the induction of NQTs relates to the visits to schools of advisers and inspectors, particularly to observe the new teacher in the classroom. This role is one that has traditionally been associated with statutory probation and was explored in some detail in the interim report of the NFER project. It was found, for example, that over three-quarters of LEAs intended to continue to send an adviser or inspector to observe new entrants, whilst just under one-fifth had no such intentions (see Appendix 1). In the six phase two case study LEAs, the number of visits made to the research schools by LEA personnel varied considerably from none throughout the whole induction year, to at least one per term.

The frequency of visits made to schools by LEA advisers and inspectors is likely to be determined by several factors. Perhaps the most important will be the extent to which schools value this service and are prepared to 'buy it back' with their delegated funds. This was an important question to which several case study schools had already given attention. Where funds were still predominantly held centrally by the LEA, a significant factor was the degree to which the LEA continued to see school visits and classroom observation as an important part of its role. As more and more LEAs concentrate resources and efforts on such activities as bidding for OFSTED inspections it may be that less importance will be attached to this traditional role. In several LEAs, observations of NQTs did not occur unless a specific request was made by the school.

In one of the case study LEAs with a large number of grant-maintained schools, a choice of three services to schools had been offered. In relation to the induction of NQTs secondary schools were able to purchase one of the following:

- a general (or link) inspector would monitor all NQTs in the school and this would involve a number of visits and observations. During visits enquiries would be made about the NQT's progress, confirmation (with the head) that the school's observation programme was being carried out and that monitoring by the professional tutor was operational

- an appropriate subject specialist inspector would observe each NQT, again consisting of one or more visits and observations over the induction year

- a combination of the above.

Both secondary schools involved in the research project from this LEA - one grant-maintained and the other LEA-maintained - opted for the first service level agreement. The specific costs of the above arrangements were not mentioned for the LEA school but they were for the GM school. The induction managers in both schools spoke highly of their respective link inspectors and the importance of involving them in the induction process. The 'outside' or objective view that the LEA person could provide was most welcomed and both schools intended to continue to make use of that service in the following year.

An Example

The grant-maintained school involved in the NFER research had six NQTs who were the responsibility of a senior teacher. She explained that the school had been approached by at least five neighbouring LEAs offering their induction services but this year they had decided to continue to make use of the host authority. It would only be if the school felt *'we were not getting good value that we'd be prepared to go elsewhere'*. The induction manager commented that previously, under probation, the visits of the school's link inspector were used to check on her own and colleagues' observations:

> *I found it very useful. So we're buying him in (for two days in February) and he will observe all the NQTs. It's also a useful check on me and the HoDs. In the past we've had one or two fail probation, so it's been necessary and useful.*

During the second interview it was stated that the pastoral or link inspector had visited the school and seen all the new teachers in their classrooms. The inspector had observed lessons, debriefed each NQT and spent several hours with the induction manager. At this stage (mid-Spring term) it was the intention to use the inspector's comments to complete the LEA's report forms on each NQT. (At this school the reporting or assessment arrangements were completed by the end of the second term with NQTs becoming part of the appraisal system from the third term onwards.) It was felt that there was no need for the LEA inspector to do further observations or visit them again in the summer. However, there had been some concerns expressed about one of the NQTs so the inspector was invited back for a further observation. This second observation took place in the summer term during which time the inspector asked to see several of the NQT's lessons. During the earlier visit the inspector had observed a difficult Year 10 class. For the second visit he wished to see this same group as well as one of the teacher's favourite classes. This was done on two separate days in the same week during which the inspector took the opportunity to observe another NQT who had started in the new year. The inspector's comments were such that it was decided to put the NQT on 'extension' and to continue to provide support next academic year, possibly involving the subject specialist adviser.

In general, schools made use of and highly valued the wider expertise and experience of subject and link inspectors and advisers for monitoring purposes, and to ensure that the school's judgements about a new teacher's performance were fair and reasonable. This was especially the case for primary schools where NQTs were not usually appointed every year. A primary head explained how difficult he would find it without support from the LEA for a judgement which affected future careers - *'pitching your judgement is a real problem especially if you haven't had an NQT for some time'*. Another primary head in the same LEA spoke of the value of an external perspective from the school's adviser, regardless of subject or phase background:

> *(its) someone who comes in with a level of objectivity, who you can relate to quite easily - his judgements are valued highly. He's unthreatening, he'll listen, cares about people, looks at classroom relationships, relates well to young children. ... the NQT feels she's lucky to have that kind of support. His judgements are highly valued.*
> (Headteacher: Primary.)

LEA personnel were seen as making a distinctive contribution as impartial, informed outsiders. An induction manager suggested that with the possible demise of the LEA, senior colleagues from other schools might be employed in this capacity but added *'advisers have the assurance of a certain professional neutrality'* and presumably would therefore be very difficult to replace. Others did not see higher education personnel as being in a position to perform this role.

This quality assurance function of the LEA was not utilised in several of the case study schools. These induction managers made it clear that the services of the LEA adviser or inspector would only be called upon if it was thought the NQT was experiencing difficulties which the school was unable to resolve. In probationary terms, the teacher was deemed to be 'at risk' and possibly would 'fail' the induction period.

So much for the school's use of LEA personnel - but what about the NQTs themselves, what value or worth did they derive from actually being observed by individuals from outside the school? Generally, responses were very positive. Although not looking forward to their visits and being rather apprehensive about them, the vast majority of NQTs who had been observed by LEA personnel remarked how helpful the verbal and written comments received had been. As with observations undertaken by school colleagues (see Chapter 5) NQTs were very appreciative of any feedback they obtained on their own classroom performance and for suggestions regarding what needed to be done to improve practice. As with induction managers, several NQTs made reference to the unique 'neutral' or 'outsider' role of the adviser: *'Someone who doesn't know you as a person with a wider view of many schools', 'someone who is impartial; there to help to choose concerns for you to focus on... the adviser has seen so many different practices and has a long history in education. It's the independent person assessing you.'* Interestingly, several NQTs remarked that the necessary critical edge that they obtained from LEA advisers and inspectors was sometimes missing from in-school observations, partly, it was suggested, because of the effect such 'criticism' might have on working relationships.

Where NQTs expressed dissatisfaction with the adviser's or inspector's visits, this invariably focused on how the observation had been **managed.** In one school the adviser's visit had been re-arranged four times so the NQT concerned noted there was no longer any point in planning for this. In some other schools, NQTs were unhappy when they felt insufficient time had been allocated to enable adequate feedback to be given. In one case the mentor rebuked herself for not providing the NQT with cover to enable a proper debriefing to occur, whilst in another school an NQT who had been observed for six periods (four with the same class!) was very critical of the fact that so little time had been set aside for feedback:

I did have a feedback session with him straight after (during lunch) but it was rather hurried and from my point of view rather unsatisfactory. It was a bit of a struggle having somebody sitting there watching you for six periods. I would've liked a longer feedback session, half an hour wasn't enough. He had taken copious notes during the six period observation but we were able to have very little discussion of these. We really didn't get to discuss very much ... I did find (all) the observations beneficial but with the inspector's visit I think he could have spent less time observing me and perhaps more time giving me feedback.

(NQT: Secondary.)

Criticism from advisers was not well received when given without reference to any positive features observed. An NQT in a different school remarked that she was only given 15 minutes for feedback after an observation and **all** of this time was used in discussing only what was wrong with the lesson.

This greatly upset the NQT and she had to be reassured by the mentor *'that things were not quite as bad as had been made out'*. The NQT remarked on the potential damage of such criticism to a teacher of only 12 week's experience. At the end of the first term NQTs can be particularly low in morale and self-esteem and the NQT felt outside observers should be aware of this. The mentor also commented that the incident emphasised the importance of leaving the NQT with something positive – *'the adviser had been oblivious of the impression he'd left with her'*. Fortunately, the responses to the adviser's final visit, when the choice of focus was decided by the NQT, was much more positive. On this occasion the mentor was concerned to ensure that observation time was matched with equivalent time for debriefing.

Finally, it is worth noting that there were mixed views about the artificiality of classroom observations. For some they were seen as false, one-off, contrived affairs whereas others did not see observation as necessarily 'a special show'. One secondary NQT used the analogy of the term's teaching as a film and described it as *'an edited shot for him to see - it's not a lie'*. (She also saw it as an opportunity in post-observation discussion to justify what had been attempted and to use the adviser as a source of new ideas.) Interestingly, several NQTs remarked that classroom observations - whether undertaken by school or LEA personnel - were of more benefit when greater risks were taken and the observer invited to look at the NQT's more challenging lessons and classes. Obviously, these invitations were more likely as NQTs gained confidence and competence.

The training of mentors/induction managers

As part of the first phase of the NFER research an attempt was made to ascertain how many LEAs were offering training for individuals involved in the induction process. The interim report found that just over 70 per cent of LEAs offered some form of mentor training and preparation, although the proportion of those currently responsible for the mentoring of NQTs who had received such training varied widely both between LEAs and between school phases within the same LEA (see Appendix 1). It is probably not unreasonable to assume that this percentage figure will rise as more LEAs obtain GEST funding for induction. One of the DFE's objectives in supporting expenditure on induction training is to 'help to ensure that those responsible for induction training are effectively prepared for this role' (see Appendix 3). Indeed, with the move towards school-based and school-centred initial teacher training the role of the mentor has taken on even greater significance with the result that there are an increasing number of training courses available for those staff performing a role with trainees and/or NQTs. Courses were being offered by institutes of higher education (HEIs), LEAs or a combination of both. It was not uncommon, for example, for LEAs to work in partnership with local HE providers to offer a training programme or for the entire mentor training programme to be subcontracted to an HEI.

Several of the case study LEAs had produced guidance documents or handbooks for mentors/tutors and provided several training sessions - after school, during the school day or at residential weekends - on such matters as counselling, classroom observation, action planning and other key skills of mentoring. The mentor training provided was sometimes closely linked to the use of an LEA handbook, portfolio or profile. Mentors were introduced to the portfolio or profile and, where applicable the competences expected of NQTs, and given advice and guidance on their role in relation to its use.

In one of the case study LEAs, training had been provided for induction managers over the last three years. (In this LEA the term 'mentor' had been reserved for those who had a role with articled and licensed teachers.) The professional tutor or induction coordinator was the manager of induction but the LEA had suggested to schools (in its guidance document) that they *'may wish to consider the identification of specific members of staff to act as mentors for individual NQTs; mentors would play no part in the assessment of teachers. The role of each one is to "befriend" an NQT professionally helping in the planning, execution and self-evaluation of his or her work'*. The training was offered to primary professional tutors and funded by the LEA, and consisted of a series of six twilight sessions provided by an HEI. This had been positively received and according to one participant, *'had given me the skills I knew I would need'*. For the following year however, the LEA had asked a different HEI to provide the training. (The LEA had worked closely with this university and had offered teaching placements in its schools.)

Again the programme for professional tutors (and mentors) was to be offered after school and consisted of six sessions:

- the role of the tutor (mentor)
- supporting NQTs in behaviour management
- observing NQTs
- giving oral feedback
- skills of self-management
- continuing development of teachers.

The intention was for the training programme to be linked to an accreditation scheme. There were also plans to run a secondary programme in the near future.

Another of the case study LEAs offered a training programme for staff involved in induction as well as those who might wish to become involved in the future. This programme, held in conjunction with a neighbouring borough, was run by the local university and linked to its accreditation scheme. The short course - for both primary and secondary phases - consisted of 11 twilight sessions (each of two and a half hours duration) which were delivered by university, LEA and school personnel. The course's main aims were to support the professional development of staff working with NQTs and to enable them to develop a range of strategies to support such teachers more effectively. It also aimed to encourage a culture of reflective analysis and to deepen understanding of classroom processes that lead to constructive learning.

The programme consisted of the following sessions:
- introduction to induction: the school-based programme
- observation and feedback (2 sessions)
- the mentoring of NQTS (2 sessions)
- helping teachers to set tasks for the management of teaching and learning
- profiling, competences, proformas and the writing of reports on NQTs
- working with adults and issues of professionalism
- preparing yourself for mentoring
- the reflective practitioner/evaluation of course
- reports of teacher tutors' research/assignment work in progress

There had been a lot of interest shown in the course which was free to participants from the LEA. It was not clear how many teachers would want to complete the assignment work in order to gain credit points towards an advanced diploma.

Those interviewees who had participated in 'mentor' training programmes generally spoke in positive terms about their value. As was so often the case with any form of in-service training it was the opportunity to talk to others performing a similar role that was deemed most valuable rather than the specific course content. At least two mentors in the same LEA were unhappy with a training course they were attending after school which was funded by the LEA but run by the local HEI. In the opinion of both mentors insufficient time was being provided for the mentors to learn from each other and the course appeared *'to be being written as they go along!'* One of the mentors further remarked that little hospitality was shown – the two hour twilight sessions were held in cold uninviting rooms with no refreshments provided and *'they were not practising what they were preaching in terms of the mentoring process!'* This mentor also felt there was a need for individuals performing a coordinating or mentoring role to meet regularly with others and she would have welcomed the LEA arranging this.

Several of the case study LEAs had arranged twilight **support** meetings for their induction coordinators, mentors and professional/teacher tutors. Others had arranged support and training sessions during the day and had funded schools to enable an induction manager or mentor to be released. Unsurprisingly, the latter were better attended and it was noted that twilight sessions – be they for NQTs or their mentors were not very satisfactory: people were tired and may well have had other more pressing concerns or priorities at the time. They were most useful in terms of finding out what others were doing *('the informal dialoguing')* and for exchanging ideas and sharing practice. A mentor who had recently attended a 1.30 - 4pm session remarked:

> *The last one I want to was well attended. We really do make an effort to go to those meetings because they are so valuable, e.g. one of the group is having difficulties with one of her NQTs. She's approached the group and asked if her NQT could come into one of our schools to do some observations. So that's very useful, you can get on the phone and talk to people very quickly. The group tends to consist of DHs and senior teachers, so it's a useful network for arranging school visits.*
>
> (Mentor/deputy: Secondary.)

It was also suggested, however, that those who would probably benefit most from such support sessions simply did not attend when cover was not made available and even when it was it did not guarantee attendance.

Certainly not all those individuals performing roles in relation to induction had received some form of training or took advantage of support meetings when arranged. Training for mentors and induction managers was, however, beginning to expand and reflected the greater emphasis that was being given to school-initiated and managed induction. Increasingly, LEAs saw their role as ensuring that schools were in the best possible position to support the induction of new staff. To this end, LEAs wanted to provide helpful guidelines and supporting materials, to make clear the respective roles of all those involved in induction, to disseminate good practice and raise awareness of 'quality induction'. Some LEAs regarded the provision of profiles or portfolios (and associated training in their use) as being the central platform in assisting schools to become self-supporting with respect to induction.

Support materials and profiles

The interim report of the project had found that virtually all LEAs provided schools with written guidelines on induction (see Appendix 1) and the six case study LEAs were no exception. The documentation that they had produced for use by the schools was generally of a very high standard and many of the interviewees spoke positively of its value and quality. The following examples of the contents of such documents are taken from three LEAs - two shire counties and a London borough - the former having used some of their GEST funds 'to help improve the quality of written guidance and other materials used in the induction of NQTs' (see Appendix 3). They are offered to give an indication of the extent and range of issues and areas covered. Two of the LEAs were research case studies, whereas the third sought the assistance of the NFER, amongst others, in producing the support materials.

Examples of the contents of LEA support materials/ guidelines

Example 1: The New Teacher in School: Supporting the Work of Teachers in their Schools

This pack had been developed by the LEA in conjunction with colleagues in schools and contained the following five sections:

- guidelines for the induction and support of the new teacher - broken down into the individual responsibilities of all the different parties involved in this process

- guidance on establishing an appropriate programme of induction and support - broken down into five phases

- a personal Professional Development Profile - for completion by each new teacher which he/she will be able to use during the first year in the school

- regulations and notes of advice and guidance on reporting the new teacher's progress - including recommended reporting forms, together with specific guidance as to how and when each should be used

- blank copies of the three reporting forms which schools can photocopy as necessary.

Example 2: Taking off into Teaching

This pack had been developed by the LEA's induction coordinator with the assistance of members of the primary and secondary induction working parties. It consisted of the following sections:

- a letter of welcome from the Director of Education
- a policy statement for schools on the induction of NQTs
- the induction of NQTs
    - monitoring and assessment arrangements over the three terms
    - formal observation: principles and procedures
    - termly interim reviews: principles and procedures
- an integrated LEA/school induction programme
    - advice and guidance for NQTs:
        - before taking up appointment
        - after taking up appointment
    - induction themes for Terms 1-3:
        - in school
        - in the LEA
- professional tutor:- a person specification and job description
- responsibility of heads of department
- observation form for NQTs
    - planning and preparation
    - teacher presence and communication
    - learning environment
    - teaching content
    - lesson/class management
    - pupil response
    - subject-specific comments
    - recommendations
    - teacher's comments
- lesson/session evaluation guidelines
- interim and final review forms
    - personal
    - relationships
    - class
    - lesson/session
    - curriculum
    - identified needs

- areas for NQTs to consider:
  - personal qualities
  - professional skills
  - professional competence
  - planning and preparation
  - classroom environment
  - the language of the classroom
  - control/discipline
  - assessment
  - relationships
- the school file and your personal file

Example 3: The First Year of Teaching

This document had been produced, using GEST funds, by a team of primary and secondary school heads and deputies seconded during a term. It consisted of the following sections:

- introduction
- the induction of NQTs
  - managing the induction process
  - implementing the induction
- a competence based approach to professional development:
  - introduction
  - the identification of competences and associated criteria
- the professional development profile:
  - introduction
  - the profile
- mentoring:
  - a definition
  - effective mentoring
  - training needs
  - meeting the challenges
  - a checklist for mentors
- bibliography
- appendix
  - school management and personnel policies

Induction profiles and competence-based approaches to the identification of individual NQT needs were becoming more common as exemplified in the last example. Again, the impetus behind such developments was often GEST funding and the DFE's objective to 'improve the links between ITT, induction of NQTs and INSET during the early years of teachers' careers, particularly through the development of profiling and competence-based approaches to professional development' (see Appendix 3). There is currently much debate about the competences required for teaching and whether or not there is a need for a **nationally** agreed profile of skills or competences. The two most recent government documents on secondary and primary teacher training have specified the competences which trainees should have achieved on the completion of training but have stressed that they 'do not purport to provide a complete syllabus for initial teacher training' (GB. DFE, 1992). Even more recent developments suggest that such profiles should be based on a common framework and the Secretary of State intends to ask the Council for the Accreditation of Teacher Education (CATE) to give him initial advice on the preparation of guidance on profiles of competence for teachers (GB. DFE, 1993). At the time of the research there was considerable variation between the different types of profile being used, with some detailing competences and their associated performance criteria, whilst others were more open-ended and less prescriptive allowing the participants a greater say on the appropriate criteria for profiling.

In the six case study LEAs, profiles and portfolios were being used with new teachers to varying degrees:

- two shire counties had developed and were using competence-based profiles

- a metropolitan borough had devised and piloted separate portfolios for its primary and secondary NQTs

- a London borough had used a pre-appointment personal profile to identify the main components of NQTs' training along with their strengths and areas for further development

- a metropolitan borough had made no moves towards profiling (it was making use of a proforma for use with classroom observation)

- a London borough had made a decision not to develop a competence-based profile but had produced an induction portfolio for NQTs.

Since the completion of the research the last mentioned LEA has, interestingly, decided to pilot a competence-based profile. It has, however, decided not to 'reinvent the wheel' and produce its own but rather to fine tune and contextualise a profile that has already been developed. In fact the profile it intends to pilot is one which has been successfully marketed by another of the case study LEAs.

So what do these profiles and portfolios look like, how are they used with NQTs and what was the reaction of schools to their use? It is the intention of this final section to answer these questions by reference to the case studies.

Although not directly found in the case studies, the earlier NFER questionnaire survey for the interim report identified a number of LEAs who were using GEST funds to develop profiles building on and refining the so-called 'CATE competences' (i.e. those outlined in Circular 9/92 on secondary initial teacher training). Several LEAs in the north west, for example, had been working with a university faculty of education to produce competence-based profiles and these are now publicly available for other schools and LEAs to purchase should they so wish (Smith and West-Burnham, 1993).

The two case study LEAs with competence-based profiles had devised their own sets of competences. Working parties had been established by LEA personnel with representation from both primary and secondary schools and local HEIs. The CATE competences were published during this time and both working parties were able to use them to ensure that there were no obvious areas of omission. In one LEA the professional development profile (and associated competency criteria) was part of a support pack (see Example 1 in earlier section), whereas the other LEA had produced a self-contained document entitled 'The New Teacher Competency Profile' (for further details of how this was developed see Gifford, 1993. The competence statements informing the profile have, with permission of the LEA, been reproduced in Appendix 4). A brief summary of the two documents follows which shows the different approaches taken. The third example - again produced by a group of LEA, HE and school personnel (including NQTs), largely as a result of a two-day residential - was not competence-based and used the term portfolio rather than profile. There are differences between profiles and portfolios - the latter usually expects evidence of performance to be collected - but essentially both are attempts to devise instruments that can be used by NQTs, usually in conjunction with their mentors, to reflect and to act on that reflection to improve practice. They are used to document progress and achievement, and structure the process of self-review whilst helping identify individual training and development needs. (For an analysis of their use with teacher trainees see Murphy *et al*, 1993; and with school managers see Earley, 1992.)

Example 1: Professional Development Profile
- Introduction
  - what is a profile for?
  - what are competences?
- Personal information
- Competency criteria
  - level 1: more than satisfied with performance/understanding
  - level 2: satisfied with performance/understanding
  - level 3: less than satisfied with performance/understanding
- Use of above criteria to reflect on:
  - the school (10 elements)
  - subject expertise (4 elements)
  - management of learning (10 elements)
  - assessing, recording and reporting progress (12 elements)
  - further professional development (6 elements)

Example 2: New Teacher Competency Profile
- The aim of the competency profile
- Principles of the profile
- The profile in school and the mentor's role
- The profile: initial discussion, review targets and action plans
- Guidance notes: how to use the profile
- Unpicking competency statements:
  - curriculum knowledge and planning (7 elements)
  - classroom management (11 elements)
  - assessing, recording and reporting (8 elements)
- Loose leaf appendices:
  - tracker/year planner
  - competency menu cards
  - competency stickers
  - answers to some of your questions

Example 3: NQTs in Secondary Schools: Portfolio

- Introduction
- An outline timetable of provision for NQTs
- Personal data sheets:
  - personal details
  - initial training details
- Job data sheets:
  - job description and teaching duties
  - school calendar and INSET needs
- Review sheets (each contains a list of issues to stimulate thinking and writing)
  - establishing and developing relationships (7 issues)
  - planning and preparation (8 issues)
  - classroom management (7 issues)
  - teaching and learning (10 issues)
  - professional activities outside classroom (6 issues)
- Targets and actions plans (for each term)
- Classroom support visit - guidance notes. (Each NQT is entitled to at least one visit per term from mentor)
- Classroom support visit sheets (proformas)
- Record of in-service activities

Interviews with school personnel in the above three LEAs included questions relating to the use and value of the profiles and portfolios which had been developed. In the first LEA, the professional development profile - part of a wider support pack for schools with new teachers - had not yet been extensively used or made available to all schools. Where it had been used it was regarded as a most useful self-assessment tool that would link in very well with staff appraisal. It was used initially by the NQTs themselves and then together with the NQTs' mentors in order to identify areas for discussion, development and action. The following interview extract is taken from an NQT who had used the profile termly:

I've used the profile twice so far – the first time I used it I went through it with my mentor, but the second time I went through it on my own. After having done this last term, I said to my mentor that I was sure that I was a lot more negative now than in the first time. Perhaps it's because ignorance is bliss and you don't realise how little you know! My concern by the middle of the Spring term was whether I was making some kind of progression – I'd become more critical of my own practice - at the outset I think I was more concerned with such things as classroom organisation but I'm starting to think now about whether I'm really catering for individual children's needs? I looked at the profile over the Easter holidays. I went through all the sections of the profile but was unable to compare my responses with my initial responses. I think it was better to do it this way and then to compare your responses after you'd completed the profile for the second time. The plan is that I will have another look at the profile at the end of the summer term. Yes, the profile is something that I would recommend other NQTs to use – it's useful because it covers issues which you may not even have thought of in the first place, it makes you more aware of what you should be doing as a teacher.

(NQT: Middle.)

In the second case study LEA the competence-based profile was being used by all five schools involved in the research, in fact three of these were the schools of working party members. It should be said, however, that the positive reactions expressed by NQTs and mentors were found in all five case study schools. (The LEA had undertaken an evaluation of the profile's use in all of the county's schools. This suggested that it had generally been well-received and was seen as useful in promoting reflective development. It further stated that there was evidence that new teachers had become more effective as a result of its use and 'the competences had provided a sharper focus and the action-planning a more efficient structure'.)

The following comment was taken from a mentor in a middle school who was not involved in the production of the profile or the associated two day programme of training on its use:

I think (the profile) will be very useful once we start actually getting things written down. We've had one meeting for the initial discussion .... it's a good idea to separate the competences into three categories. It's negotiated and targets are set. We decided to focus on a couple of competences from the menu card in classroom organisation and management but in our discussion (the NQT) also wanted to look at assessment (a different menu card). So we need to get going on targets related to classroom management and then, next term, look at assessment. I think we share the ownership of the profile but ultimately it will become his. I feel it will be a most useful document and also helpful for staff appraisal. Having the list of competences could help people decide on which areas they would like observed - they provide a good starting point. (Mentor: Middle.)

It had proved difficult, however, for the mentor and the NQT to find as much time as they would have liked to use the profile. A series of events within this school, including an unusually large number of staff absences had not helped. There were plans for the profile to be used with future NQTs. Similar comments about the value of the profile were expressed by the headteacher of the other school not involved in the profile's development:

> *The profile is new. All the suggested points of discussion have been covered. She looked at these before we sat down and discussed them. Setting the targets was quite useful because we hadn't done this before - we had a lot of informal discussion after school. The areas she's highlighted as developmental areas are areas we were already working on (assessment and record-keeping were identified as targets). I'm not sure who owns the profile, so I'd be interested to know how the NQT sees this. She's been used to identifying her strengths and weaknesses through a programme (profile) which she used at college. She's given it to me to look at, so clearly she doesn't feel threatened by it. She's very open about expressing any concerns. She's seen my summary and we're due to discuss it. I hope she feels it's something we share. The new teacher package is excellent and it's made us formalise the targets.*
> (Head/mentor: Infant.)

The new teacher in the same school remarked:

> *The profile make you focus on things - weak areas that you want to spend some time on - so that's good. The idea behind it is that it's there to help me. We went through it together at first and chose some areas for development. We've agreed on some termly targets. I was concerned about record keeping, maths practical activities and progression in maths. So maths is the area that concerns me most, next term I'll focus on something else. I'm not sure who 'owns' the profile. At my college, they had a personal profile which was quite similar to the LEA's scheme. I've given mine to the head for her to look at.* (NQT: Infant.)

At the second interview she explained that finding the time to use the profile had presented some difficulties:

> *We had a meeting last week but it's the first time we've looked at it this term. There are just so many things to be done and with record keeping and the children, it's just time; time to think about it. Long term it's good to do because at the end of the year it's a catalogue of how you have been developing. It's super to have it. It should continue all the time, not just the first year. It make you think about things!*
> (NQT: Infant.)

In the other three schools in this LEA involved in the research, as might be expected, there was a very high degree of commitment to the profile. Comments from the mentors and NQTs in these schools give an indication of how valuable its use had proved to be. Most saw the profile as providing a framework or a focus to help structure one's thoughts about teaching and its component parts. The profile made NQTs - and mentors too - ask questions about what they were doing. A mentor (not a working party member) when asked in her second interview if she was still finding the profile useful remarked:

> *I think the profile is excellent and I would certainly use it again if I had another NQT. It builds in reflection. The profile gives you common ground and it is laid out there in front of you. Also it's open for you to use as you wish, there are the competences spelt out and you can use those which are most relevant to you. We will choose these together, although sometimes I've made certain suggestions to her. Some of the targets we've outlined have been fairly easy to achieve, in the short term, others it's proved to be more difficult. You have to constantly work on these and develop strategies over a longer period.*
>
> (Deputy/mentor: Primary.)

The NQT in the same school said:

> *We mostly fill in the profile together. At the end of last term we summarised and decided what we were going to focus on. We are still using the stickers in the pack. We have got together on occasions after school to discuss the profile and the areas or competences that we needs to focus on. I have found it of benefit and I would recommend the profile to be used by future NQTs, but I find a lot of the areas naturally overlap with each other and it's sometimes difficult to look at a specific area or competence. The competences are all interrelated but it's useful to get you to focus on these and to make you aware of the role of the teacher. As far as the target setting is concerned, on occasions this has been easy other times more difficult.* (NQT: Primary.)

A head of department in another school welcomed the structure and guidance that the profile offered:

> *I think that anything that helps to channel what we're supposed to do and gives it a bit more structure and guidance is to be applauded. I have felt a bit at sea in the past – we go in, we observe and it's been a bit unstructured. The profile provides us with that structure - I've observed the NQT twice. I made a concrete decision not to formally observe her until after half term. The DH and the NQT decided upon which competences they were going to look at. The NQT and I then met and discussed it. We decided to look at classroom management and she targeted three areas on the menu cards. So we sat down and discussed No. 5 – I felt her beginning and endings of lessons were already excellent! We discussed looking at those areas. I saw a Year 8 class last Friday specifically to look at those areas of competence. I produced and typed up a list of general comments. We unpacked what the competences actually meant. ...At the end of the exercise I felt it was very productive to brainstorm that together but I do think the process of brainstorming or discussing is beneficial for bringing things out. I'm sure it's helpful for the mentor as much as for the NQT. The problem, however, is one of time to do this. I've got one NQT, if I had more I don't know how I'd cope. It's a questions of fitting it in. I'd like more time to do this properly.*
>
> (HoD/mentor: Secondary.)

This middle manager and the NQT went on to use the profile flexibly - they did not restrict themselves to the competences specified on the menu cards. The fact that the profile could be adapted to meet identified needs was seen as a further advantage. The NQT, when asked at the third interview, said she intended to continue to use the profile in her second year. It was suggested that if teachers were used to using a profile *'then a lot of the fear associated with appraisal is removed'*. The induction manager in this school saw the use of the profile as being of particular benefit to middle managers: their experiences of identifying areas of competence with NQTs was helping with the appraisal process and for managing other teachers in their department.

In the third and final case study LEA which had developed a profile or portfolio the reactions were more mixed. Some insights were offered by an NQT at the beginning of his second term in post:

The idea is good but sometimes it sounds too vague, I don't always see the point of filling in bits of paper when I can talk about it to someone, yet it might be a jog to your memory. If you were isolated, didn't see or talk with other teachers, then it could be good, an on-going record of how we felt, what we're doing. Filling it in can be unnecessary because the issues you're talking about in the portfolio are the ones you're constantly talking about with teachers. It's of more use to someone not in the school, who came in to see how we felt we've developed over the year. It's important not to deify the actual document, it's just a means to an end. Many aspects of the portfolio and induction from the LEA were at their most important when you're in a bad situation, when nothing is working, there's no system of support and appraisal, no forum for bouncing ideas around. (NQT: Secondary.)

The deputy head in the same school, who had been involved in helping develop the portfolio, remarked that its completion should not be seen as an imposition or *'as just something else to fill in'*. A view which it was felt was held by some NQTs, whilst others were not entirely clear for what purpose it was being completed. It should be seen as *'a means to an end: to help with reflection'* but to quote the same NQT at the time of his second interview:

A lot people were rather irritated by the process of having to fill in more documents, after a day at school the last thing you want to do is write it all out again. The aim of it was acceptable; people were concentrating too much on what's on paper, rather than listening to you. The day to day discussions with the department cover the issues of NQT's development [well enough], so there was a lot of criticism of this rather abstract document which a lot felt they were only filling it in because it had to be filled ... not that they were against thinking, criticising or analysing - they were just irritated by the medium. I agree it's a bit laborious. (NQT: Secondary.)

The new teacher went on to remark that, in his view, those who made most use of the portfolio tended to be those NQTs who were receiving least support. The portfolio was a document to refer to, part of a process and not the end product. It provided an opportunity to set and agree targets. This could be achieved without a profile or portfolio but its existence *'ensures targets are set and things are monitored in some schools where they might not be done otherwise'*.

An induction manager in another school, also involved in the development of the portfolio, spoke negatively about it and how it was on *'the very bottom of the list of (the NQT's) priorities'*. The exercise was seen very much as being paper-driven and not reflecting NQT's concerns. This deputy remarked that the consensus view of other mentors he had spoken to at their most recent meeting *'was that it wasn't useful'*. However, the portfolio had been adapted in the light of criticisms received and the deputy remarked that the following year's NQTs would be making use of it.

Within the same LEA, primary NQTs were the responsibility of a different officer and a separate profile had been developed in conjunction with a different HEI. Comments regarding the use of this document in schools centred around it 'long-windedness' and degree of detail, the time that was needed for its completion and the fact that it was too similar to a student profile, not treating the NQT as an adult professional. A head remarked that *'the requirements of the profile made everyone feel guilty that they were not filling them in'*.

Primary NQTs on the other hand spoke more positively of the value of the document and how *'it broke everything down into sections ... which made you stop and think'* or *'gave you ideas for (the mentor and I) to think how I'm progressing in the classroom'*. The most valuable parts of the document were *'the tick-lists, the suggestions and the information packs'*. It helped to prioritise what was needed and to give an indication of what was required in terms of development. It was felt, however, to have become *'decreasingly useful'* over the year. The action planning part of the profile was also seen to be beneficial but there was a similar concern about *'just writing things down for their own sake'* and the need to write out lesson plans. Again, as a result of feedback received from primary school mentors and NQTs, the profile had been revised for the following year and the process streamlined.

CHAPTER 10
MANAGING INDUCTION IN SCHOOLS

Investing in people

It will be recalled that the 30 schools involved in the project had been identified for the researchers as schools where the induction of NQTs was given importance and was generally believed to be well-managed. Not all of the case study schools had induction policies - about one-third had a specific induction policy, whilst a further third were in the process of producing one or had subsumed induction within a more general staff development policy. However, for some heads and deputies, what happened 'on the ground' was of more importance than having a policy *per se*, although there was a general recognition that things were more likely to happen if *'they were written down and part of an NQT entitlement or right'*. It was said to be useful to have a policy statement or document as this had to be agreed by senior managers and the governing body and was therefore more likely to be able to secure the necessary resources. In addition, there needed to be arrangements for evaluation to take place to ensure that the training and induction support provided by the school and LEA was meeting the needs of the NQT and the school. To this end, most schools and LEAs had various evaluation procedures in place and although most were rather informal or unsystematic, there were attempts being made to evaluate practice in order to improve the situation for the future.

The case study schools demonstrated a strong commitment to induction, indeed to staff development generally. Senior managers wanted a positive attitude and approach to staff development and training to infuse all areas of the school including their work with new teachers. Several heads and deputies spoke of 'investing in people' and being prepared to commit the necessary resources to staff development, including induction, so as to demonstrate that commitment. A well-designed induction programme of support was seen as providing a proper foundation from which to build. For some induction managers such a commitment had to be given a high priority because *'if you make a hash of it, it's somebody's career that suffers.'* Devoting resources to induction was seen as a long term investment: *'We were prepared to give of our time..., that shows our investment'*, which will, hopefully, *'pay dividends in five years when the good grounding/nurturing given to NQTs now will be ploughed back into support for others in the profession'*. Schools, it was said, had a professional responsibility to NQTs (and students) to ensure they were given a good start or base.

Ultimately, the success of a school was said to depend on high quality teachers who were well-motivated and committed. As a primary head remarked: *'teachers are your most important resource - if they're good then so is your school'*. Unless new teachers felt valued in the school it was said they would not perform well in the classroom. It was therefore important *'to facilitate mechanisms to support NQTs'* and senior managers perceived a major role to be facilitation and resource allocation, thereby creating the conditions to ensure that staff felt valued and were able 'to deliver in the classroom'. The purpose of investing so much time and energy was not only to increase the chances of NQTs being *'more effective in the classroom'* but also *'to try and make sure our way of working is generated through them and that they don't operate in their classrooms in a totally different way to that of other teachers.'* NQTs were therefore seen as an investment but one which, at least on first appearance, required *'a fair whack of valuable resources!'*

Resource management

As might be expected, resources and their management was frequently raised as a crucial issue in managing induction. Senior managers were quickly learning the basics of budgeting and spending - as one induction coordinator remarked: *'we've gone from capitation (only a few years ago!) to local management and (in some cases) GMS. We're becoming much more cost conscious.'* With self-management and local management (LMS) schools had a greater say in how financial decisions were made and senior managers were conscious of the resource implications of employing NQTs. Recent reports from HMI (GB. DFE, HMI, 1992) and the Audit Commission (1993) have pointed to the growing trend for schools and governing bodies to employ NQTs rather than more experienced teachers. The headteachers involved in the research stated that NQTs were appointed if they were 'the best candidates'. They referred to the need for 'fresh blood and new ideas' or to reduce the age profile of the staff. In only one school was it stated that an NQT had been appointed (for the following year) in order *'to save money'*, although elsewhere an induction manager noted how, in his view, headteachers in these budget-conscious days *'were more concerned with meeting short-term budget deficits, than the long term interests of the profession.'* In the case study schools the appointment of NQTs was **not** seen to be a means of saving money or 'a cheap option.' It was said that any new entrant to the profession had to be given adequate support, such as a reduced timetable, an induction programme, exemption from pastoral or cover duties, or regular access to a mentor. All of these had significant resource implications. By the time these **'entitlements'** had been taken into account, along with the deployment of senior management time, there was said to be little or no difference between the financial costs of employing an NQT or a more experienced teacher. In fact in one school it had been calculated to cost more to employ an NQT, especially if they began to experience problems and required additional support.

Resource management was also said to be about priorities and competing claims on the budget. The induction of NQTs could not therefore be reviewed in isolation. A school's induction programme of support always had to be balanced with other needs and priorities, and had to be married to the school development plan. It was recognised, however, that devoting resources to staff development and induction was 'money well spent' as *'demotivated staff are not cost-effective.'* Schools could ill-afford to have teachers who were not seen as assets. Similarly, if NQTs were not given the support they needed, any problems experienced would eventually have to be resolved by the school's senior managers. Negative feedback or parental complaints about NQTs, for example, had eventually to be dealt with by heads and deputies themselves.

When senior staff were asked how the induction of NQTs was funded it was generally apparent that monies had not been set aside or earmarked for specific activities. In the past schools may have been entitled to funding from the LEA to support additional non-contact time or to attend LEA induction days but the situation was rapidly changing. In some cases central funds were still available for certain LEA activities (e.g. cover for induction 'days' or mentor training) but increasingly such funds were being devolved to schools and, to a greater extent, earmarked for induction purposes. Heads and senior management teams were therefore attempting to manage their budgets of which funds for staff development and training - including induction - would be considered along with competing claims. In general, the larger the school (i.e. the more pupils) the bigger its budget and the greater flexibility it therefore had to deploy its resources.

A recent report from the Audit Commission states that, on average, 70 per cent of schools' budgets was spent on teachers' salaries and suggests that the way in which schools manage this was the most important factor in the management of the budget (Audit Commission, 1993). However, the variation between schools in the proportion of schools' budgets which was spent on teachers' salaries was quite wide. The Audit Commission report suggests that some schools have scope to re-prioritise resources should they so wish. 'Schools of similar size and levels of funding may spend quite different proportions of their budgets on teachers. It may be appropriate for a school to spend either 60 to 80 per cent of the budget on teachers' salaries - indeed an aim of local management is that schools should exercise discretion in deploying staff' (Audit Commission, 1993). It is not known if this variation was reflected in the NFER case study schools but it was in the degree to which induction was resourced. Although all of the heads and deputies spoke of their school's **commitment** to induction and staff development there were considerable differences in how that support for NQTs was funded. Two primary schools in the same case study LEA clearly illustrated this point. In one school the head explained that they were *'pushed to the absolute limit and were carrying an overspend.'* They were therefore unable to provide non-contact time for the mentor or NQT, although all staff were given 30 minutes per week during assembly (taken by the head) for team meetings. The NQT in this school had a full teaching load although some time had been created for him to observe other classes and visit another school. (Supply cover had been purchased or the head had taken the NQT's class.) In the other primary school, the mentor who was also the deputy head, did not have a full-time class. The head, when appointed ten years ago, had made the decision to increase class sizes and this had enabled the deputy to no longer have a class of her own. She was therefore able to work alongside colleagues - both recently appointed and more experienced - in the classroom. As such, the NQT in this school received considerable classroom support from the deputy head/mentor although the NQT was not given any additional non-contact time to that received by other teachers in the school. The mentor was due to retire at the end of the academic year but her successor was to continue to be a 'non-teaching' deputy who would work closely with next year's NQT. Both primary schools in this LEA demonstrated a strong commitment to induction but clearly were able to resource it to varying degrees. Similarly, a headteacher of another primary school in a different LEA, spoke of a considerable budget underspend which would be used to maintain a level of support to NQTs; this included one-half day's release from teaching duties.

It was not common for induction managers and mentors to be given 'extra time' to undertake their responsibilities with NQTs. Induction coordinators and professional/teacher tutors - who, as shown in Chapter 4, were invariably senior managers - were expected to carry out their induction duties as part of their wider responsibilities. In some cases these were very extensive, whereas in others 'induction' might constitute only one of several school-wide responsibilities. In one secondary school, for example, the induction coordinator was also responsible for staff development and INSET, staff appraisal, ITT, Year 7 and the science and design faculties. As the head remarked *'the deputy is very conscientious...but is it possible to do it all well, especially if you have four or five NQTs?'* In another, induction had become the responsibility of a senior teacher who worked closely with a deputy who had overall responsibility for staff development, INSET and appraisal. In this school, each of the three deputies had two or three senior teachers working with them and the induction coordinator - who taught a 60 per cent timetable - was also in charge of ITT.

Middle managers with NQTs and primary school teachers with mentoring responsibilities were not usually given additional non-contact time in specific recognition of this. Job descriptions usually included reference to the need to support and develop staff, including newly-appointed teachers, although as research into middle managers has shown this is often an aspect of the job that is not readily embraced (Earley & Fletcher-Campbell, 1992). Similarly, mentors (if not senior or middle managers) did not usually receive extra time (or remuneration) for their work with NQTs. Several heads made reference to how they expected staff to show a 'professional commitment' to their colleagues or spoke of the professional development (and career) opportunities that working with NQTs (or trainees) would bring. (See Chapter 6 for a more detailed discussion of the amount of time given to mentoring.)

The challenges of induction

It was perhaps unsurprising that when induction managers were asked (at the time of the second interview) what issues were most challenging in the management of induction, numerous references were again made to the need to find sufficient time in order for all those involved *'to do the job properly'*. Interviewees spoke of *'snatched time'*, *'the lack of quality time'*, their *'inability to devote enough time'* to NQTs and of the concerns they had about whether they were *'giving the best to the person you're responsible for.'* References were made, for example, to how so much depended on 'good will' and of meetings arranged in teachers' 'own time'.

More specific problems raised were:

- the difficulty of obtaining regular supply teachers to replace NQTs when they attended LEA induction sessions
- organising school visits for the NQT
- the need for cover for observations as NQTs and their mentors taught at the same time

Several induction managers made reference to the challenge of working with a mixed ability group of middle managers, some of whom needed constant reminding of their responsibilities with NQTs.

> *All my best laid plans fall down if the HoDs don't do what they're supposed to do! It's not that they don't care or can't be bothered it's that they don't have the (people) management skills. In the words of one of our NQTs 'it's as if you've given him a list and he goes through it every week'. Ineffective HoDs usually say 'let's stick to the lessons if you've any other problems, you can go to the (induction coordinator).*
> (Professional tutor: Secondary.)

There was said to be a greater need for more formal links and consistency between those performing a mentoring role within the school, especially as the direct contribution of the LEA towards induction continued to diminish.

For others, the major challenge in managing induction centred on meeting NQTs' needs or developing them, particularly *'when there were signs that all was not well'*. It was generally agreed to be much easier working with capable and confident teachers than it was with the less competent.

> *The challenge to me is developing the individual but trying to do it in a way that they feel some allegiance to the school and try and put something back.* (Induction coordinator: Secondary.)

> *I'm fortunate to have an able NQT. It would be quite a challenge if there'd been problems... (nevertheless) the main challenge is whether I'm stretching him far enough. I don't know whether I am.* (Mentor: Primary.)

> *The main challenge is one of balance – of giving NQTs quality personal support so that they can go out there and do the job...giving them the professional input they need to be good teachers. It's most challenging working with people who aren't strong – it's much easier working with people like (the NQT) who are very professional in their approach and who are keen to develop and progress* (Teacher tutor: Secondary.)

Several requests were made from induction managers for more guidance on how to help those NQTs who were 'not quite as good'. The struggling new teacher was seen as a major issue for schools in the future as LEAs were unlikely to have the resources to deal with this matter as they had previously. The key question that was raised was whether schools would be willing or able to devote the extra time and resources to those new teachers who were having difficulties. The growing trend towards appointing NQTs on short term contracts was noted as being a reflection of this situation. A trend which some induction managers noted with concern.

Several respondents remarked how they found it difficult - and thus a challenge - to be able to observe the classroom practice of NQTs and **not** to be overly critical of that practice.

> *It's having to say things which I would prefer not having to say! Or to focus on things which are somewhat delicate. At the end of the day you are talking about a person who is obviously doing their very best. If they were able to do things better then presumably they would. So you're dealing with a person who has feelings, etc. But of course you also have the responsibility to the children; their needs must be paramount. You try to be constructively critical and to promote self reflection, you have to promote the person as they are and how they've dealt with the situation. It may not be your way but it's how they've handled the situation.* (Mentor: Primary.)

I think in order to improve people's practice you should never be negative and yet I've learned that when you've been a Head a long time, like I have, when you go into another classroom, if you're not careful all the things that are not right strike you. It's very tempting to say why aren't you doing so and so, what about this or that? In fact that's a very bad model to work to because any experienced teacher can go into another's class and spot what's wrong. That's the nature of primary teaching things are never perfect. It's more a matter of wanting to support people, it's helping to support people without undermining them. (Headteacher: Primary.)

Views from NQTs

Those who had responsibility for the management of induction in the case study schools sought feedback from their NQTs with a view to improving, where possible, the support and training programme that was being planned for NQTs in the following year. As part of the research the NQTs were asked, at the time of the third and final interview, to comment on which particular aspects of their induction they had found most helpful, how practices within their schools might be improved and what advice they would give to new teachers starting their first job. It is the intention of this final section to summarise briefly these data and thus provide further insights into what NQTs themselves regarded as effective practice. However, it should be remembered that the NFER sample of new teachers was small and it is therefore not known how representative these views were of NQTs in general.

It is perhaps unsurprising to find that those NQTs in the research who were given one-half day release or additional non-contact time frequently made reference to this as being **the most helpful** aspect of their induction year. Although a clear need for time away from class was identified it was interesting that the NQTs spoke of how that time had been used over the year in response to their **changing** needs. References were also commonly made to the LEA induction programme and the importance of having opportunities to meet other NQTs. Support from mentors and heads of departments was also mentioned but several NQTs made specific reference to the support and advice they received from staff generally. The accessibility of staff and the fact that *'doors were always open'* was of significance.

It is worth noting that in response to this question several NQTs made reference to the need for a second mentor and to the importance of links with teachers who had recently completed their first year or who were not *'too far removed from the experience'*. Such teachers were perceived to be *'more in touch with the issues and problems you're likely to face'*. Less frequently mentioned but significant nevertheless were references to school visits, feedback from classroom observations and residential conferences (although these were very few in number they obviously made a considerable impact). For several NQTs, however, it proved impossible to distinguish a **single** aspect of their programme of support as it had all been helpful, albeit in different ways.

As for advice to next year's group of NQTs, the most common response was to suggest that new teachers should not be afraid to ask questions and seek the views of others. As one commented: *'you must scream and make yourself heard...you have to tell them (if you've problems) they're not mind readers!'* There was a need to be actively involved - effective induction was negotiated not imposed. It was felt essential to become a team member and work hard at developing good relations with colleagues. A number of references were also made to the importance of being well-organised and a good manager of time - areas which were said to be inadequately covered either during initial training or induction. Finally, reference was made to the optimum use of the summer period and for the need to make the most of the induction and support offered by the school and LEA. Already most of the NQTs were painfully aware that their second year in post was likely to be at least as demanding, if not more so, as that induction 'cushion' was removed.

CHAPTER 11
SUMMARY AND CONCLUDING COMMENTS

Summary

In April 1992 the NFER project *The role of the LEA in the professional development of new teachers* commenced. It was funded through the NFER's Membership Programme, lasted 18 months and consisted of two research phases: firstly, a questionnaire survey of LEAs; and, secondly, case studies of schools and LEAs. An interim report, based on the survey of LEAs, was published in the autumn (Earley, 1992) and its main findings have been reproduced as Appendix 1. The aim of the second phase of the project was to focus on a small number of 'good practice' schools and LEAs in order to gather data from the main participants, especially newly-qualified teachers (NQTs), on their experiences of the induction process over the course of the NQTs' first year in post. This was achieved by the researchers visiting each of the case study schools on three separate occasions during the academic year, 1992-93. It is this documentary and interview data derived from the 30 nominated case study schools in six LEAs which have informed this research report on effective induction practices.

It is the intention of this final chapter to summarise the key findings of the research - thus providing a reasonably succinct overview which could be used by schools to help inform their own practices - whilst also offering some brief concluding comments. It is **not** the intention, however, to make recommendations or to discuss NQTs' entitlements or *'initiation rights'*. The views of LEA personnel on these matters were considered in the interim report and they have also been extensively examined by the teacher associations (e.g. Thompson, 1993), by the emergent *General Teaching Council for England and Wales* (Calderhead and Lambert, 1992), the *School Teachers Review Body* (GB. STRB. 1993), and, most recently, by the *National Commission on Education* (1993). A recent edition of the *British Journal of In-Service Education*, (Vol. 19, No. 1. 1993) devoted exclusively to induction also has several articles on this theme and an editorial looking back over the 20 years or so since the publication of the James Report.

Key findings from NFER research on NQT induction

The following section provides a summary of the key research findings of the NFER project with reference (in brackets) to the relevant chapter where a more detailed discussion can be found.

Characteristics of Effective Induction (Chapter 2)

- It is flexible and negotiated; not imposed or pre-determined.
- It meets teachers' needs (training, development, social and psychological).
- It is part of a school-wide approach to supporting all staff (a climate of mutual support and development).
- It is systematic and planned, and includes:
  - links to specific individual(s)
  - programmes of classroom observation and feedback
  - opportunities for regular contact with other NQTs (within and outside school).
- It encourages reflection on practice (usually with a mentor).
- It enables staff to become active and valued members who can contribute to the school and its development.
- It lays the foundation for a life-long professional career.

Models of Induction Support (Chapter 2)

- Six main arenas of support for NQTs were identified:
  - LEA induction programmes
  - LEA adviser/inspector visits
  - School induction 'programmes'
  - Mentor arrangements in schools
  - Mentor training and support groups
  - Documentation, handbooks and profiles.
- Four main models of induction support emerged from the case study schools:
  - Mono-support systems
  - Bi-support systems
  - Tri-support systems
  - Multi-support systems.

Initial Experiences (Chapter 3)

- Induction was mentioned for most NQTs during the course of their ITT and about one-half of NQTs noted that induction was an important factor when applying for positions.
- Most schools offered unstructured and informal pre-appointment (summer) programmes.
- Just under one-half of NQTs had experienced 'culture shock' which, for others, had been alleviated by productive use of the summer period.
- All the case study NQTs were able to visit their schools during the summer, albeit to varying degrees.
- Formally structured summer induction programmes were found in only 3 schools.
- Most NQTs worked at least a 50 hour week.

School Induction Programmes (Chapter 4)

- Responsibility for induction was usually within the remit of senior staff. Induction managers in primary schools were also more likely to act as mentors but doubts were raised about the capacity to take on both roles.
- Over one-half of the sample had been induction managers for only 2 years or less and operated in one or more of the following modes:
  - arranging a central induction programme
  - undertaking individual sessions with NQTs
  - undertaking observation for assessment
  - coordinating mentor activity
  - ensuring the NQT's induction entitlement.
- Central induction programmes were found in all 12 secondary schools but only 3 of the primary schools. There was considerable variation in the timing of these meetings (most occurred after school) and the duration of the central programme. The content of the secondary central induction programmes (Table 4.6) mainly covered the themes of:
  - pupil learning e.g. differentiation
  - teaching strategies e.g. flexible learning
  - the administration of learning e.g. parent reports
  - pastoral roles e.g. form tutoring
  - school context e.g. governors
  - wider curriculum e.g. cross-curriculum
  - NQT needs e.g. time management
  - induction issues e.g. use of profile.

- NQTs had individual sessions - often with a specific focus on observation - with induction manager. These were more common in primary than secondary schools.

- Primary NQTs with non-contact time often negotiated an individualised programme of development, and their induction managers generally played a low key role where there were effective mentoring arrangements in place.

School Induction: Assessment and Entitlements (Chapter 5)

Observation for assessment

- Observation procedures ranged from the formal (with agreed procedures) to the very informal - with the latter being more common in primary schools.

- The number of times NQTs were formally observed by their *induction managers* varied:
    - one-fifth of the sample was not observed at all
    - one-tenth were observed in *each* of the 3 school terms.

- All secondary NQTs were formally observed by school personnel (induction manager and/or mentor), whereas 4 primary NQTs had no such observation. Far more primary than secondary NQTs had a single observer (rather than several) within the school looking at their teaching practice.

- When visits by LEA personnel were included, no secondary NQT was 'judged' by only one 'classroom assessor', whereas nearly one-third of primary NQTs were without a second opinion on their teaching. Some primary NQTs were uncertain as to whether they had been assessed and, in some cases, were disappointed that they had not received formal or official feedback on their classroom performance. All secondary NQTs saw formal observations and feedback as beneficial, particularly when used with a profile.

- The availability of time and people were frequently mentioned as factors preventing formal observation and feedback from occurring. All case study schools gave (or stated they would give) greater attention to those NQTs who were defined as experiencing problems. This would usually involve LEA personnel. Some induction managers raised concern about the diminution of the LEA's role in relation to observation and assessment.

- It was evident that schools did not always have the time, resources or intent to assess NQTs' performance in the classroom.

- Consistency between schools in their observation procedures was not at all apparent.

- The training needs of secondary middle managers for their induction role was largely unfulfilled at either school or LEA level. Only 2 of the 12 secondary schools had instituted formal 'training' for their mentors. (Both schools were using a competence-based profile.)

NQT entitlements

- For induction managers an important part of their role was to 'protect' NQTs and/or 'guarantee' entitlements. NQTs' entitlements could consist of any (or all) of the following:
    - no cover
    - no form tutor role or curriculum responsibility
    - reduced timetable or half-day release.

- In the 18 case study primary schools:
    - 7 offered their NQTs a weekly half-day release
    - 3 offered their NQTs occasional release
    - 8 offered their NQTs the same amount (if any) of non-contact time as other staff.

- In the 12 case study secondary schools:
    - 9 offered NQTs extra non-contact time (varying from $\frac{3}{4}$ hr to $2\frac{2}{2}$ hrs per week)
    - 3 offered no extra non-contact time.

- The ways in which NQTs made use of extra release or non-contact time varied considerably. For some, it was seen as time to be used for such things as marking and preparation *(amelioration)* rather than for *professional development* opportunities (e.g. observation and school visits). Primary NQTs tended to use their release time rather more for developmental purposes than their secondary counterparts.

- Secondary induction managers held different views about the efficacy of giving NQTs responsibility for a form tutor group and approached it differently. Similar variations were found in relation to cover duties.

- Primary NQTs were generally not asked to take on a curriculum or subject responsibility in their first year (although examples were found, especially in the foundation subject areas of art and PE, and where NQTs showed particular ability). There were expectations by both senior staff and NQTs that a curriculum leadership role would be embraced in year 2.

Mentoring (Chapter 6)

- An analysis of personnel undertaking an official mentoring role with NQTs showed that:
  - in secondary schools mentors were almost always line managers (HoDs and deputy heads)
  - in primary schools mentors ranged from headteachers to ex-probationers.
- 8 factors were mentioned when choosing a mentor:
  - recent experience of being an NQT/probationer
  - proximity (teaching in nearby classroom)
  - direct linkage/overlap with NQT teaching commitments, expertise/experience directly relevant to NQT
  - non-connection with an assessment (or direct line-manager) role/function
  - a source of accurate information about school/department procedures
  - a valuable role model
  - capacity to effect change in school on NQTs' behalf
  - ensured commitment to/investment in the role.
- Mentoring was most comprehensively and conscientiously undertaken when mentors could identify one or more of the following benefits to themselves:
  - professional development
  - career advancement
  - 'psychic reward' or personal satisfaction
  - institutional strategic advantage (e.g. to facilitate change).
- The time and timing of mentor support was found to vary:
  - in 5 of the 12 secondary schools and 4 of the 18 primary schools, discussions time was timetabled in term 1
  - 8 of the primary schools defined regular mentor presence in the NQT's classroom as a major component of induction/support
  - in both primary and secondary schools mentors reported spending less time with NQTs as the year progressed and the new teachers grew in confidence and capability
  - despite the commitment of mentors there were often serious difficulties in finding the time to sustain their developmental role with NQTs as non-contact time was rarely offered to mentors specifically for their induction role.

Mentoring in Action (Chapter 7)

- 6 main types of modes of mentor activity were identified:
  - mentor as classroom support
  - mentor as classroom analyst
  - mentor as collaborative planner
  - mentor as induction programme negotiator
  - mentor as informationist
  - mentor as welfare monitor.

- Each mode of mentor activity may contribute to the *amelioration*, *development* and *assessment* of NQTs, although tensions could emerge when one person attempted to undertake *all* these aspects of induction. It was rarely expected that a single person would provide the full range of mentor roles or modes of mentor activity. *Collective mentoring* was a more accurate term to describe how induction responsibilities were undertaken.

- The most consistently mentioned attribute of mentors was the *ability to listen*, although other qualities, such as giving time, showing genuine interest, being supportive, honest and approachable were also frequently noted.

LEA Induction Programmes (Chapter 8)

Benefits gained

- Within the 6 case study LEAs there was considerable variation in the number of days NQTs were entitled to attend a central induction programme. NQTs generally found the programmes valuable, although their usefulness varied according to the NQTs' previous experience and training.

- Induction managers valued the LEA programmes for such reasons as:
  - access to specialist knowledge and up-to-date information
  - expertise in the training and development of teachers
  - offering a perspective that went beyond the school
  - cost-effectiveness, consistency and coherence
  - time away from school for reflection and development and to counteract potential insularity.

- NQTs frequently mentioned factors related to the programme's *relevance* and *practical applicability* in the classroom. Other key factors were:
  - the quality of the provision
  - the degree to which more pressing concerns were given priority.

- There was seen to be a need to provide opportunities (quality time) for NQTs to meet (preferably outside of school) with other NQTs. It did not matter so much how and when such meetings took place just so long as they actually occurred.

The need for differentiation

- Given the wide range of background, age and experience of NQTs it was increasingly important to identify NQTs' needs (both individual and collective) and to offer *differentiated* and *negotiated* induction programmes. Flexibility and responsiveness were seen as crucial.

- NQTs frequently made reference to the benefits of meeting with their peers, especially outside of the school. It was not always the *content* of the LEA programme that was the crucial factor: social and emotional support, reassurance and the sharing of ideas were also highly rated.

- NQTs' needs or '*stages of concern*' changed from term to term, initially focusing mainly on 'survival' before turning to more specific concerns, particularly relating to the curriculum and teaching and learning. Term 2 needs often related to differentiation or assessment, whereas in term 3 the focus was often on career development and the NQTs' wider contribution to the school.

- The degree to which LEA induction programmes were coordinated with those of the school varied but there was a recognition that both should be coherent and complement each other as far as possible.

- Relevance and applicability to immediate concerns were more important to NQTs than whether or not the LEA induction programme consisted of cross- or phase-specific, subject-specific or general sessions.

Minimising disruption and costs

- Where attendance at LEA induction sessions was seen as adding significantly to NQTs' workloads - or as being increasingly difficult to fund - alternatives (e.g. residential weekends, twilight sessions) were being considered.

- Residentials, where found, were highly valued by NQTs and may become more common as 'cost-effectiveness' becomes a key criterion. (Residentials were seen as minimising disruption and reducing supply teacher costs.)

- It was recognised that for some areas and issues the LEA was in the best position to provide training for NQTs. LEAs had the requisite expertise and it would not always be realistic nor cost-effective to expect schools (or consortia) to provide the time and resources to meet these needs.

The importance of contacts

- Although the value of contacts with other NQTs was acknowledged, it was noted that the value could vary considerably according to the amount of support that NQTs received in their own schools.

- Schools were seen as being increasingly 'in the driving seat' regarding the provision of induction – including subscribing to LEA programmes – and, although the case study heads stated would continue to give priority to induction, they were not convinced that this would be the case in all schools.

Support from LEAs (Chapter 9)

Visits by LEA personnel

- The number of visits made to the case study schools by LEA personnel varied considerably from none throughout the whole induction year to at least one per term. In several LEAs, observation of NQTs by LEA personnel occurred *only* as a result of specific requests by schools.

- Schools valued highly the wider experience and expertise of LEA advisers and inspectors; some schools used them for monitoring and quality assurance purposes, whereas others would only call on their services if their NQT(s) was deemed 'at risk.'

- NQT responses to observations by LEA personnel were generally very positive - they valued particularly their professional neutrality and critical edge. Where criticism was voiced it tended to focus of insufficient time allowed for feedback.

Mentor training and support

- Several LEAs had produced documentation for mentors and induction managers as well as offering training. In some cases the training provided by LEAs was closely linked with the use of a profile. Training for mentors was becoming more common as moves towards school-based and school-centred teacher training gathered pace. Mentors and induction managers, in general, spoke positively of the training received and of the opportunities created to meet with others performing a similar role. LEAs increasingly saw their role as ensuring that schools were in a good position to support the induction of NQTs.

Profiles and support materials

- Documentation provided for schools in the 6 case study LEAs was generally of a very high standard and was valued by NQTs and their managers.

- Profiles were being used in the case study LEAs to varying degrees:
  - 2 LEAs had developed and were using competence-based profiles
  - 1 LEA had devised and piloted separate portfolios for its primary and secondary NQTs
  - 1 LEA had made use of a pre-appointment personal profile.

- In all cases (except one) LEAs had worked with HE personnel in the production of materials, using GEST funds where available.

- Profiles, where used, were regarded as particularly useful for self-assessment and staff appraisal. They provided a useful framework which encouraged NQTs - and their mentors - to reflect on their own practice.

- It was felt that profiles and portfolios should be used flexibly and adapted to meet individual needs. They were least valued when seen as overly detailed, 'paper driven' or not reflecting NQTs' current concerns. The target setting and action planning associated with profiling and portfolios was generally welcomed.

Managing Induction in Schools (Chapter 10)

Investing in people

- About one-third of case study schools had an induction policy, whilst a further one-third were in the process of producing one or had subsumed induction within a more general staff development policy. Most schools and LEAs had evaluation procedures in place although most were informal.

- The case study schools demonstrated a strong commitment to induction and to staff development generally. Several references were made to *'investing in people'* and being prepared to commit the necessary resources to staff development, including induction. Induction was seen as a 'protecting' or 'easing-in' process demanding an investment of time and resources. Schools were seen as having a professional responsibility to ensure NQTs were provided with a proper foundation from which to build.

Resource management

- Resources and their management was frequently raised as a crucial issue and senior staff were very conscious of the resource implications of employing NQTs. In only one case study school was reference made to appointing NQTs to 'save money'. Heads stated that 'the best candidates' were appointed but also referred to the need for 'fresh blood' or to reduce the staffs' age-profile. NQT appointments were not seen as 'cheap options' once their entitlements had been taken into account, along with the deployment of senior management time.

- The induction of NQTs could not be reviewed in isolation from other competing claims on the school's budget and the priorities of the school development plan. The funding of induction had not generally been earmarked but this was increasingly the case as funds were being devolved to school. Despite all the case study schools being committed to induction there was found to be considerable variation in the degree to which it was resourced.

- It was uncommon for mentors and middle managers to be given 'extra time' to undertake their NQT responsibilities. In some cases, induction managers (who were generally senior staff) had extensive school-wide responsibilities, whereas in others 'induction' might be one of only several wider responsibilities.

Induction challenges

- The major challenge in the management of induction was the need to find sufficient time for all those involved 'to do the job properly'.

- The NQT with difficulties was seen as a future major issue as LEAs were unlikely to have the necessary resources to deal with this matter as they had in the past.

- The move towards short-term or temporary contracts for NQTs was acknowledged to be a likely trend but one which several induction managers noted with concern.

Views of NQTS

- When asked about the most helpful aspect of the induction year, NQTs made reference to the extra non-contact or release time they had been allocated. This time had been used over the year in response to their changing needs.

- Other helpful aspects mentioned included:
  - LEA induction programmes
  - opportunities to meet other NQTs
  - support from mentors and HoDs
  - advice and support from staff generally
  - school visits, observation and feedback
  - residentials.

- The most commonly suggested advice NQTs would give to those entering the profession was not to be afraid to ask questions or to seek the views of others. There was a need for each NQT to be proactive in their own development and to negotiate a support programme which met their needs.

- Most NQTs were aware that their second year in post was likely to be at least as demanding, if not more so, as that induction 'cushion' was removed.

Concluding Comments

There would be little disagreement that the major outcome of induction should be a well-established and effective teacher who wished to remain in the profession whilst wanting to continue to develop. In the words of the *National Commission on Education:* 'a carefully managed induction programme is essential for creating a truly professional teacher' (NCE, 1993). Induction is perhaps best seen as part of a socialisation process – an **initiation** into both the culture of the school ('the way things are done around here') and the culture of the profession. However, there is a general consensus amongst educationists that induction arrangements are of varying quality and that the transition from initial training to fully-fledged professionalism is not as smooth as it could be. In a rapidly changing scenario of delegated budgets, devolved INSET funding, moves to grant-maintained status, the abolition of statutory probation and the changing functions of the LEA, there is a need to reconsider the respective roles of schools and LEAs in the professional development and induction of newly-qualified teachers.

Schools and LEAs are currently facing a period of transition and it is not yet clear what is likely to be the precise role of each in the induction process. Increasingly, LEAs, partly in recognition of the greater devolution of resources to schools, see themselves as supporting individual schools in their management of induction, whilst being less concerned with the direct provision of training and other services to NQTs. The production of support materials, the training of mentors and the development of profiles is tangible evidence of this trend. It could be argued that LEA central programmes are unlikely to disappear because they are seen by schools as 'adding value' to the induction process. Nevertheless, LEAs will have to adapt – indeed as has been shown, they are so doing – to this changing scenario.

There is growing evidence that schools will increasingly be prepared to purchase only those aspects of the service that they consider to be *valuable* and – in the light of delegated budgets – *cost-effective*. Whether LEAs will be able to continue to offer schools their current range of services and expertise is debatable. It should be said, however, that many of the heads and senior staff involved in the NFER project were quite pessimistic about the future role of the LEA. It was noticeable, for example, that a number made reference to how induction in schools could become more *ad hoc* as some schools decide to 'opt out of their professional responsibilities'. As the NFER research has shown, some schools – including the 30 case studies – have chosen to give induction 'the priority it deserves': how typical these 'good practice' schools are at present or will be in the future is simply not known. What is known, however, is that the quality of induction for NQTs is increasingly dependent upon *the school* and **the degree of importance which it attaches to induction.** There are fears held by some that the current OFSTED arrangement for the inspection of schools does not focus sufficiently on staff development and induction, and that there will be a need for more schools to be encouraged to monitor and evaluate their own training practices. An example of a mechanism for reviewing an organisation's training and development would be *'Investors in People'* – a government initiative that initial feedback suggests is being well-received by schools. Unlike OSTED inspections, however, there is no compunction for schools to become involved in this initiative, although the introduction of staff appraisal has led to schools giving greater consideration to training and development needs, and ways in which they can be met.

Teachers entering the profession are doing so at a time of unprecedented change, not only concerning the curriculum and its assessment but also concerning teacher training and the greater role that schools play with regard to in-service training and staff development. Induction, for example, is likely to become much more closely linked with initial teacher training and some schools will become 'training establishments'. Similarly, the skills of mentoring and classroom observation acquired by teachers will be deployed in the contexts of ITT and induction, as well as staff appraisal.

Profiles, based on specified competences, are likely to become more widespread and used to inform both initial training and induction along with continuing professional development. Certainly, current GEST funding mechanisms and recent government publications suggest a continuation of this trend.

There is little doubt that some schools will be better prepared and capable of adapting to this changing scenario than others. Even in the 30 case study schools, for example, there were differing opinions expressed about the degree to which schools could provide effective staff development themselves if LEAs were to disappear. It was not necessarily the case that the large secondary schools considered themselves more independent and self-sufficient than their smaller primary counterparts. Although there was a recognition of the need to create opportunities for such things as cross-fertilisation, networking, development and training, it was not always the case that the LEA might provide these. Already some schools, especially with the introduction of school-based ITT, were developing their relationships with institutes of higher education. In turn, HEIs were increasingly offering consultancy, advisory and accreditation services to schools, in some cases – but not all – in partnership with LEAs. As some LEAs move further towards an inspectorial role, competing with others for OFSTED contracts, this trend may well continue.

Nevertheless, as the research reported here has shown, LEAs were still felt to have a major role to play in the professional development of new teachers. As the move towards **'self-managing schools'** gathers pace, it becomes increasingly obvious that some schools are more ready for 'autonomy' that others, and that there is still an important support and advice role to be fulfilled. Whether LEAs can continue to undertake that role is not clear. It should be apparent, however – and the case studies of 'good practice' used to inform this research demonstrate this only too clearly – that the LEA, working in partnership with schools, can effectively support the management of school-initiated induction and the professional development of teachers. If LEAs do disappear it has been said that there will be a need to reinvent them. At the very least something similar will be needed to perform the crucial role of supporting schools and preventing insularity and 'the recycling of inadequacies'.

It is only relatively recently that there has been a proper recognition that a school's most important resource is its staff and that 'investing in people' is an effective route to school improvement. It is hoped that the research reported here provides useful data and important insights into the induction process from which both schools and LEAs will be able to examine their own practices. There would be little disagreement that **the quality of the teaching and learning process for pupils** largely depends on the quality of the school's teachers. This in turn is largely dependent upon schools being **well-managed**, where staff development and training is taken seriously and conditions created which enable *both* staff and students to achieve effective learning. If staff – both teaching and non-teaching – are not 'learning' there is less likelihood that this is the case for students. A **'learning organisation'** is one which subscribes heavily to a developmental culture and gives training and development a high priority. As such, induction is perhaps best seen as part of staff development generally.

Without doubt, effective induction practices mean *'never having to say you're sorry you got the damned job'*, but, most importantly, they also provide a proper foundation for a career where learning and development are considered to be on-going. Hopefully, the NFER research report illuminates the nature of effective induction practices and will be of some value to those schools (and the LEAs supporting them) who are or wish to become 'learning organisations'. A consideration of induction practices for new staff, including NQTs, might therefore be a useful starting point.

REFERENCES

AUDIT COMMISSION. (1993). *Adding up the Sums: Schools' Management of their Finances.* London: HMSO.

BOLAM, R., BAKER, K. and McMAHON, A. (1979). *The Teacher Induction Pilot Schemes (TIPS) Project: National Evaluation Report.* Bristol: University of Bristol, School of Education.

BROWN, S. and EARLEY, P. (1990). *Enabling Teachers to Undertake In-Service Education and Training: a Report to the DES.* Slough: National Foundation for Educational Research.

CALDERHEAD, J. and LAMBERT, J. (1992). *The Induction of Newly Appointed Teachers.* London: General Teaching Council Initiative for England and Wales.

DRAPER, J., FRASER, H., SMITH, D. and TAYLOR, W. (1991). *A Study of Probationers.* Edinburgh: Heriot-Watt University, Moray House Institute of Education.

EARLEY, P. (1992). *Beyond Initial Teacher Training: Induction and the Role of the LEA.* Slough: National Foundation for Educational Research.

EARLEY, P. (1992). 'Using competences for school management development', *British Journal of In-Service Education,* 18, 3, 176-85.

EARLEY, P. and FLETCHER-CAMPBELL, F. (1992). *The Time to Manage? Department and Faculty Heads at Work.* London: Routledge.

GIFFORD, S. (1992). 'Surrey New Teacher Competency Project', *British Journal of In-Service Education,* 18, 3, 159-65.

GREAT BRITAIN. DEPARTMENT FOR EDUCATION (1992). *Initial Teacher Training (Secondary Phase)* (Circular No.9/92). London: DFE.

GREAT BRITAIN. DEPARTMENT FOR EDUCATION. HER MAJESTY'S INSPECTORATE (1992). *The Implementation of Local Management of Schools. A Report by HM Inspectorate. 1989-92.* London: HMSO.

GREAT BRITAIN. DEPARTMENT FOR EDUCATION (1993). *The Initial Training of Primary School Teachers: New Criteria for Course Approval* (Draft Circular). London: DFE.

GREAT BRITAIN. DEPARTMENT FOR EDUCATION AND WELSH OFFICE (1993). *The Government's Proposals for the Reform of Initial Teacher Training.* London: DFE.

GREAT BRITAIN. DEPARTMENT OF EDUCATION AND SCIENCE (1992). *Induction of Newly-Qualified Teachers* (Administrative Memorandum 2/92). London: DES.

GREAT BRITAIN. DEPARTMENT OF EDUCATION AND SCIENCE. HER MAJESTY'S INSPECTORATE (1992). *The Induction and Probation of New Teachers, 1988-1991* (HMI Report 62/92). London: DES.

GREAT BRITAIN. OFFICE OF STANDARDS IN EDUCATION (1993). *The New Teacher in School: a Survey by HM Inspectors in England and Wales 1992.* London: HMSO.

GREAT BRITAIN. PARLIAMENT. HOUSE OF COMMONS (1993). *School Teachers Review Body: 2nd Report 1993* (Cm 2151). London: HMSO.

HARLAND, J., KINDER, K. and KEYS, W. (1993). *Restructuring INSET: Privatisation and its Alternatives.* Slough: NFER.

JAMES REPORT. GREAT BRITAIN. DEPARTMENT OF EDUCATION AND SCIENCE. COMMITTEE OF INQUIRY INTO TEACHER TRAINING (1972). *Teacher Education and Training.* London: HMSO.

NATIONAL COMMISSION ON EDUCATION (1993). *Learning to Succeed: Report of the National Commission on Education.* London: Heinemann.

MURPHY, R., MAHONEY, P., JONES, J. and CALDERHEAD, J. (1993). 'Profiling in initial teacher education', *Journal of Teacher Development,* **2**, 3, 141-46.

SMITH, P. and WEST-BURNHAM, J. (1993). *Mentoring in the Effective School.* Harlow: Longman.

THOMPSON, M. (1993). 'The weakest link: ATL's proposals', *British Journal of In-Service Education,* **19**, 1, 12-15.

APPENDIX 1
Executive Summary of Interim Report

- In April, 1992 the NFER commenced an 18-month research project to investigate the role of LEAs in the professional development of new teachers.

- As part of this project a questionnaire was sent to all LEAs in England and Wales in June, 1992. Returns were received from 72 LEAs which, along with accompanying documentation, provide the information for this report, the first of two to be produced by NFER.

- Professional development is an on-going process although a distinction is made between initial teacher training, induction and in-service education. Induction – the main concern of this interim report – is defined as the process enabling new teachers to become effective.

- Recent developments in education have meant LEAs are reconsidering their roles and functions and wish to know how best to support newly-qualified teachers and ensure a smooth transition from ITT, through induction to continuing professional development.

Main Research Findings

Induction policies and guidance

- Just over three-quarters of LEAs had a written policy statement on induction of NQTs, while only a quarter required schools to have a written policy.

- Virtually all LEAs provided schools with written guidelines on induction.

- Nearly two-fifths of LEAs and schools provided funds for pre-appointment visits, whilst one-fifth funded pre-appointment LEA visits and introductions.

Induction programmes

- All LEAs arranged a central (and/or area-based) induction programme and over three-quarters saw this as an important incentive for NQTs when applying for posts.

- There was considerable variation between LEAs in the number of days each new teacher was entitled to follow an induction programme.

- LEA induction programmes were seen as particularly valuable in providing opportunities for NQTs to meet and share experiences in a neutral setting. They also helped ensure cost-effective inputs and were able to take a broader perspective than would be possible within an individual school.

- All induction programmes included opportunities for NQTs to observe classes in their schools, whilst the vast majority enabled visits and observation in other schools to take place.

- LEAs supported school-initiated induction primarily by providing support materials and advice, structured classroom observation, the monitoring of practice and the training of mentors. Most saw their supporting role changing in the future in the light of delegated budgets, devolved INSET funds and the abolition of statutory probation.

- Just over 70 per cent of LEAs offered mentor training and preparation, although the proportion of those currently responsible for the mentoring of NQTs who had received such training varied widely both between LEAs and between school phases within the same LEA.

- Nearly eight out of ten LEAs had arrangements in place which avoided unnecessary duplication between LEA- and school-initiated induction, and few respondents thought their induction programme did not match the needs of individual teachers.

- In only about one-fifth of LEAs did induction programmes discuss links with the wider community and business.

- Just under two-thirds of respondents thought the induction period for new teachers should last for 12 months.

- The majority of LEAs rated their induction programmes as 'good' or 'more than satisfactory'. These judgements were often based on LEA evaluations undertaken with NQTs and others.

The assessment of new entrants

- Eight out of ten respondents did not agree that probation should be abandoned or that it had become a 'meaningless reality'.

- Over three-quarters of LEAs still intended to send an adviser or inspector to observe new entrants in the classroom and virtually all had plans to continue to offer advice and support.

Links with ITT institutions

- Two-fifths of LEAs described the partnership with local ITT establishments as 'quite well' or 'well developed', with a further fifth regarding it as 'not at all developed'.

- A variety of pilot schemes to develop and improve links were found, usually GEST-funded.

- Very few authorities involved ITT institutions directly in the induction process, although several were seeking its accreditation.

- Nearly nine-tenths of respondents felt there were areas of competence not adequately covered during initial training. The most common area mentioned was classroom management and organisation, followed by the management of pupil behaviour and discipline.

Continuing professional development

- Many LEAs were developing competence-based profiles, often in conjunction with ITT institutions. Others had shelved all development work which was seen as unrealistic in the present climate.

- Records of achievement and professional development profiles were seen as eventually forming part of appraisal systems and personal target setting or development plans.

- About three-quarters of all LEAs were in favour of a nationally agreed profile of skills or competences for teachers on the completion of training, at the end of their first year in post, and at the end of the early phase of their career.

- It was suggested that this profile of skills or competences should be devised by the profession itself. LEAs, schools, ITT institutions and the professional associations all had a role to play.

Conditions of service and professional entitlements

- About sixty per cent of respondents thought that most schools within their LEA did not offer new entrants a reduced teaching timetable.

- About one-third of LEAs offered guidance to schools on the percentage of contact time for NQTs.

- Advice to schools on the provision of non-contact time for the mentor was offered in about six out of ten LEAs.

- The most frequently mentioned component of a new entrant's minimum professional development entitlement was a reduced timetable or a period of non-contact time. (The amount suggested varied from ten to 30 per cent.)

- Other minimum entitlements commonly mentioned were regular sessions with a trained mentor; the opportunity to be observed and to observe others and visit other schools; access to external advice and support; a planned induction programme and the opportunity to attend appropriate training.

- New entrants were seen as having a right to properly managed support structures in schools and LEAs. These should be monitored and evaluated.

- About one-half of LEAs regarded their current arrangements as 'meeting most' or 'meeting all' of the identified minimum entitlements.

Other issues and concerns

The majority of respondents saw LEAs as continuing to have a significant role in relation to the induction and support of NQTs. However, recent developments militated against this and further marginalised their role.

The LEA of the future was advised to focus its resources on one or more of the following areas:
- mentor training
- developing links with ITT institutions
- supporting and monitoring school-initiated induction
- providing LEA induction programmes.

Of these four areas the development and training of mentors (and others with staff development or induction roles in schools) was by far the most commonly mentioned.

Concerns were expressed about the levels of funding for induction, the need to ensure all NQTs received at least a minimum amount of induction training and support, and the degree to which schools would give priority to induction.

(Earley, 1992.)

APPENDIX 2
Establishing a programme of induction and support for the new teacher

The process of induction is considered as one which begins at the moment of appointment and continues throughout the first year of teaching, with the focus of support changing over time. It is, therefore, important to evaluate the process at the end of each phase. The nature and type of support required may be described in phases. The phases describe positive steps where a new teacher is integrating successfully into the work of the school. Where there is cause for concern, a headteacher should be considering seeking personnel advice sometime during phase 4.

Phase 1

The phase begins when the new teacher is appointed to the school. At this time the school should be able to provide relevant information in the form of:

- a diary with term dates and major schools events;
- a staff handbook or similar document giving useful facts about the school's curriculum, organisation and management, staff structure, staff training and development policy, discipline, extra-curricular activities, relationships with the community and other relevant information;
- notice of the timetable to be taught;
- all curricular documents, including statutory documents, relating to the National Curriculum and relevant to the subjects to be taught;
- information about equipment and other resources available;
- information about the planned programme of induction and support provided by the school and the LEA;
- the competency based profile.

Every encouragement should be given to the newly qualified teacher to visit the school during the latter part of the term when college courses have finished. The school may consider employing the new teacher for a negotiated period. Teachers already employed within the LEA are entitled to paid leave to visit their new schools following interview and prior to taking up their new posts. There may be further opportunities to share in end of term INSET initiatives. Joining arrangements will need to be established.

This is also a time when the pastoral needs of the new teacher may be addressed, including possible accommodation and travel requirements.

Introduction may be made to the mentor, who may wish at this time to exchange addresses and telephone numbers and to arrange to meet before the start of the new term.

Phase 2

This may be seen as a period of adjustment for the new teacher as he/she joins the staff of the school in his/her first teaching appointment.

Before the beginning of term the new teacher will need to have details relating to, for example:

- the geography of the school;
- the class/es to be taught and related details;
- the range of available resources together with systems for their retrieval;
- information not previously given relating to school procedures, etc.

The new teacher's training area should be adequately equipped for the start of term. Once term has started it is important that the new teacher has:

- some protected non-contact time for professional use;
- opportunity to discuss, on a regular and supportive basis, progress with his/her mentor;
- a break during the day and especially at lunchtime;
- opportunity to mix socially with staff.

Phase 3

This is a period of developing relationships – throughout the first half term – as the new teacher settles into the routine of daily school life.

It is a time when the school will be particularly alert to the specific needs of the new teacher building on his/her previous training and experience.

During this time, the new teacher will need to become familiar with his/her new class/es, teaching areas and the philosophy of the school.

In this context, the school may choose to address a number of questions including:

- what arrangements are being made for the new teacher to observe other key practitioners either this term or in future ones?
- what time might be available for supported self-reflection?
- are there issues relating to the new teacher's classroom practice that should be addressed?
- when might the mentor be released to work alongside and observe the new teacher?
- how frequently should de-briefing take place?
- what role does the headteacher fulfil in the new teacher/mentor relationship?

New teachers should continue to be given guidance with each new event. Other opportunities should be taken, as and when appropriate, to introduce the new teacher to the school's wider network of relationships.

Phase 4

Phase 4 is a period of consolidation, lasting as it does up to the beginning of the final half-term of the induction year. Meetings between the new teacher and mentor should continue.

During this period, the new teacher may need support in developing aspects of teaching which may be identified in the Professional Development Profile. In-service expectations and opportunities may be identified and opportunities taken to implement them.

Increasingly, the new teacher should be encouraged to become involved with school initiatives by, for example, capitalising on areas of expertise, but not to the detriment of the development of teaching skills. As the new teacher gains confidence and becomes more competent within the classroom he/she should be encouraged to become more involved in the wider aspects of school life.

Phase 5

At the end of the induction year, it is important that the new teacher continues to receive support as required. This may be particularly the case, for example, where reports/profiles are to be completed or where there are specific school events.

The new teacher should be encouraged to review his/her Professional Development Profile and may choose to share it.

At this point in the year it would be appropriate to identify achievements and plan for continued professional development.

The mentor and new teacher should evaluate the programme of induction and support of the past year and inform senior management as appropriate.

(Reproduced, with kind permission, from *The New Teacher in School: Supporting the Work of Teachers in their Schools*. Hampshire LEA, 1993.)

APPENDIX 3
The Department for Education's objectives for induction training

The Department's objectives in supporting expenditure by LEAs and GM schools on induction training are to:

- improve the links between initial teacher training, induction of NQTs and INSET during the early year of teachers' careers, particularly through the development of profiling and competence based approaches to professional development;

- improve coordination between the induction activities of LEAs and those of schools;

- encourage provision which is carefully differentiated to meet the particular needs of individual teachers and groups of teachers who will have obtained qualified teacher status through a variety of different routes;

- help to ensure that those responsible for induction training are effectively prepared for this role;

- help to improve the quality of written guidance and other materials used in the induction of NQTs.

(Admin. Memo 2/92. 11 August 1992.)

APPENDIX 4
Competence statements

CURRICULUM KNOWLEDGE AND PLANNING

1. Plans work using knowledge of school policies, schemes of work and National Curriculum requirements in the long and short term.
2. Plans differentiated work allowing progression and continuity.
3. Communicates clear learning objectives supported by appropriate activities to meet the needs of individuals and groups.
4. Takes account of the social and emotional needs of pupils.
5. Plans to manage pupil behaviour.
6. Works as a member of a team, planning co-operatively, sharing information, ideas and expertise.
7. Where appropriate, consults and plans with learning support staff and outside agencies.

CLASSROOM MANAGEMENT

1. Organises the working environment appropriately from the range of activities taking place.
2. Maintains a stimulating, informative environment displaying pupil's work appropriately.
3. Ensures that resources are readily available and organised to facilitate learning.
4. Trains pupils to take responsibility for resources and the environment.
5. Uses a variety of suitable teaching and learning styles.
6. Gains and holds pupil attention through verbal and non-verbal strategies.
7. Ensures that the beginnings and endings of sessions and transitions from one activity to another are smooth.
8. Gives instructions, explanations and feedback which are clear, unambiguous and helpful.
9. Communicates personal enthusiasm and stimulates learning interest.
10. Conveys an understanding of the work and a clear expectation of outcomes.
11. Varies strategies to manage appropriate and inappropriate behaviour to sustain a purposeful working atmosphere.
12. Uses praise to reinforce effort and achievement ("Catch them being good").
13. Monitors pupil response and achievement and uses this information to promote individual development.

ASSESSING, RECORDING AND REPORTING

1. Assesses pupils' work effectively, using positive, formative methods and regular feedback.
2. Uses a variety of modes to assess pupils' learning according to National Curriculum requirements and school/department policies.
3. Actively involves pupils in the assessment process.
4. Uses assessment to identify individual needs.
5. Keeps records of pupil's progress and achievements in line with school policy.
6. Reports pupil achievement according to statutory requirements and school policy.
7. Consults, informs and advises parents about their children's learning and development.
8. Uses assessment for self evaluative future planning.

Reproduced, with kind permission, from *The Surrey New Teacher Competency Profile*, Surrey LEA, 1993.